EVERMAY

# GEORGETOWN
# HOUSES

## OF THE
## FEDERAL PERIOD

WASHINGTON · D · C ·

1780～1830

★ ★ ★

*By* · DEERING · DAVIS · A · I · D ·
STEPHEN · P · DORSEY · &
RALPH · COLE · HALL

*Foreword by*
NANCY · McCLELLAND · A · I · D ·

BONANZA BOOKS · NEW YORK

# FOREWORD

INVITED BY THE AUTHORS to sponsor this work on "Georgetown Houses," the American Institute of Decorators accepts the honor with pride and pleasure, believing that the book will prove to be an important contribution to the architectural history of this country.

Illustrated here are twenty-two houses just one mile from the White House and leading hotels of Washington. With travel curtailed, interest in everything American increased by our National crisis, and the Capital crowded with people from every part of the globe, this book should serve a valuable purpose by presenting, in well-documented form, an account of part of our heritage that is too little known.

Although the pages that follow are concerned primarily, indeed, with one exception, exclusively with Georgetown, its personal history, and its architecture after 1780, it does not seem amiss in this foreword to say a few words about the family relation of Georgetown to our National Capital. For Georgetown in a manner was the parent city of Washington.

The little town first came into National prominence in 1783, when Congress, weary of moving about from New York to Philadelphia, to Trenton, to Baltimore, to Lancaster and York, to Princeton and Annapolis, decided to fix on a permanent residence for the Capital. At the outset a location on the Delaware was selected. Two weeks later it was decided that, in addition, there should be a second National Capital, *"at or near the lower falls of the Potomac at Georgetown."*

This idea of the two Capitals was not received with great enthusiasm. Francis Hopkins flicked it with a sly touch of ridicule by proposing that the statue of Washington which was authorized at the same session be put on wheels so that it could follow wherever Congress went!

Seven years later Georgetown learned that the plan of one Federal City had finally been adopted; that it was to be on the Potomac and that the President of the United States himself was coming to view the proposed site with his three commissioners.

In his diary Washington records using Suter's Tavern as his Georgetown headquarters, and makes note of several visits there. He first came from Mount Vernon on October fifteenth, 1790, and set out with his commissioners and the principal citizens of the town to inspect the surrounding country. The following year in March he visited Georgetown again. Major L'Enfant, who was to lay out the new city, had arrived on March twelfth, as noted in the Georgetown Weekly Record. Andrew Ellicott, the official surveyor, was also there.[1] Washington's Diary describes the great occasion:

*March 28, 1791.* Breakfasted at Georgetown about 8; where having appointed the commissioners under the residence law to meet me, I found Mr Johnson, one of them (and who is Chief Justice of the State) in waiting—and soon after came in David Stuart and Dan'l Carroll, Esqs, the other two. A few miles out of Town, I was met by the principal citizens of the place and escorted in by them; and dined at Suter's tavern, (where I also lodged) at a public dinner given by the Mayor and corporation—previous to which I examined the surveys of Mr Ellicot, who had been sent on to lay out the district of ten miles square for the Federal seat: and also the works of Majr L'Enfant, who had been engaged to examine and make a draught of the grds. in the vicinity of Georgetown and Carrollsburg on the Eastern branch, making arrangements for examining the ground myself tomorrow with the commissioners.

[1] Records of the Columbia Historical Society, Vol. II, 1908.

Then came the President's proclamation about the decision on the permanent seat of Government; the "Ten Miles Square" authorized by Congress had finally been selected. The proclamation concludes;

*Done at Georgetown aforesaid, the 30th day of March, in the year of our Lord 1791, and in the independence of the United States the fifteenth.*

*By the President*

*Thomas Jefferson*                    *George Washington*

Work on the Federal City began October 12th, 1792, when the cornerstone of the President's House was laid, without any special ceremony. James Hoban, the architect and builder, advertised for "good carpenters and joiners at two dollars per day at the President's House." When Washington laid the cornerstone of the Capitol in his capacity of a Mason the following September, the Mayor and Corporation of Georgetown were at the head of the procession.

The Capital, however, at this time was a city only in name, and for many years was obliged to rely upon Georgetown for its living accommodations, its supplies and its social life. There is ample evidence of this in the correspondence of the senators and representatives after Congress moved to Washington in 1800. John Cotton Smith in a letter to his wife recounted; "A large proportion of the Southern members took lodgings at Georgetown, which, though of a superior order, were three miles distant from the Capitol, and, of course, rendered the daily employment of hackney coaches indispensable."

Oliver Wolcott, Secretary of the Treasury, soon after arriving in the Federal City wrote; "There are few houses in any one place, and most of them small, miserable huts, which present an awful contrast to the public buildings. . . . You may look in almost any direction, over an extent of ground nearly as large as the City of New York, without seeing a fence or any object except brick kilns and temporary huts for laborers." Again, in a letter to his wife, Wolcott said; "I do not perceive how the members of Congress can possibly secure lodgings unless they will consent to live . . . crowded ten or twenty into one house and utterly secluded from society. The only resource for those who wish to live comfortably will be found in Georgetown, three miles distant, over as bad a road in winter as the claygrounds near Hartford."

Georgetown newspapers and the National Intelligencer of Washington were at this time full of advertisements of lodgings, addressed to the Congressmen. The Georgetown Mansion House even went so far as to print an announcement from its enterprising owner that, "for the accommodation of such members of Congress as may favor him with their patronage he will keep horses and carriages to convey them to and fro Congress Hall *free of expence.* (sic)"

Gouverneur Morris of New York, reaching Washington after days of bumping along bad roads, sent this spicy letter to Princesse de la Tour and Taxis; "We only need here houses, cellars, kitchens, scholarly men, amiable women, and a few other such trifles to possess a perfect city, for we can walk over it as we would the fields and woods. . . . I hasten to assure you that building stone is plentiful, that excellent bricks are baked here, that we are not wanting in sites for magnificent mansions . . . in a word, that this is the best city in the world to live in—*in the future!*" Morris added that, as he was not "one of those good people whom we call *posterity,*" he would meanwhile certainly prefer to live somewhere else.[2]

It would seem that the President from the very beginning desired government workers to establish themselves in Washington proper, rather than in Georgetown. His note sent on May 17th, 1795, to Alexander White, one of the Commissioners, says rather severely: "I shall intimate that a residence in the City, if a house is to be had, will be more promotive of its welfare than your abode in Georgetown."

Such warnings must have been repeated, for a year later the Commissioners informed the

[2] Diary of Gouverneur Morris, Vol. 2. pp. 394-5.

President that they intended to establish themselves in the Federal City "as soon as ever decent houses could be had."

It is not difficult to understand the partiality of Government members and their families for quiet comfortable, beautiful, well-bred old Georgetown. In contrast with the swampy ground of Washington, its dreary wilderness of open fields, its few scattered dwellings and the crowded boarding houses on Capitol Hill, the ordered comfort of the small city across Rock Creek was a blissful refuge. "From the steps of the Capitol," says Claude Bowers, describing the Federal City in his Jefferson and Hamilton, "one could count seven or eight boarding houses (Jefferson lived in one of them) one tailor's shop, one shoemaker's, one printing establishment, the home of a washwoman and a grocer's shop; a stationery store, a drygoods house and an oyster market. And this was all." A vivid picture of Washington in the year 1800!

Georgetown, on the other hand, had been in existence for almost a hundred and fifty years. Its foremost citizens "were not men of wealth in the present acceptation of the word, but they were men of birth, education, high character and influence for good in the community, and their wives and daughters were women of charming personality and greatest refinement. Together with their near neighbors, they constituted a society sought by the most cultivated and distinguished in the public and private life of the Capitol." [3]

\*  \*  \*  \*  \*  \*

Georgetown is a city of brick. The abundance of good clay on every hand, made it the natural building material to use for homes. There are many indications that claypits were dug on or near the sites where houses were to be built, and brick-yards established there. The same procedure was followed in Williamsburg, you will remember.

The Reverend Francis Makemie, first Presbyterian minister to arrive on the Eastern Shore of Maryland, wrote a book descriptive of the country, which was published in London early in the eighteenth century. "Here we have a clear and serene Air," he said, "a long and hot summer, a short and sharp winter, a free and fertile soil. . . . Here are vast quantities of Timber for Shipping, Trade and Architecture. . . . Here are in most places Bricks to be made at every man's Door for building." [4]

Bricks made in Virginia in the seventeenth century were rated at eight shilling a thousand. In England between 1650 and 1700 they could not be purchased for less than eighteen shillings a thousand. Had they been sent over for use in the Colonies, transportation across the ocean must have been added to this price, as well as import duties.

Mr. George A. Townsend's article on "Houses of Imported Bricks" written for the Records of the Columbia Historical Society sheds light in a very interesting manner on the old discussion about home-made versus imported bricks. He cites the fact that in 1695, "good brick clay having been found in the neighborhood of Annapolis, contracts were made with Casper Hermann, a burgess from Cecil County, for the erection of the Parish Church, Schoolhouse and State House." In Virginia in 1736, a contractor named George Dudley "Doth agree, for satisfaction of four years servitude, to make Isham Randolph one hundred thousand bricks and to set and burn them." [5]

The great abundance of clay on the Eastern coast may be attributed to the country's geological structure, which is that of an old mountain range, steadily eroding toward the ocean. This wash has taken the top soil off the level bench, from the foot-hills to the fall-line, leaving a band of soil better suited to brickmaking than to agriculture. East of the fall-line is the extensive tidewater area, with deep alluvial soil containing no stones but plenty of good clay.

[3] From "Old Homes on Georgetown Heights," by William Gordon.
[4] From "A Plain and Friendly Perswasive to the Inhabitants of Virginia and Maryland for Promoting Towns and Cohabitation, by a Well-Wisher of Both Governments," reprinted in the Virginia Magazine of History and Biography, Vol. IV.
[5] George A. Townsend in Records of the Columbia Historical Society, Vol. 7, pp. 195-210.

In Georgetown many of the old brick sidewalks and brick street-gutters still exist. And among the beauties of the place, in addition to the dwelling-houses, are the high brick walls smothered with ivy, which surround the lovely gardens.

The bricks used in these constructions are larger than those made today and they are set in a special way which is well described by Arthur Holden and Lewis A. Coffin, Jr.,[6] who say, in writing of Annapolis Houses: "The brickwork is most interesting from many points and of great import to an architect. The color of the brick approximates a dull salmon and is distinctly different from the brick-color found anywhere else in the country. It is very agreeable to the eye, giving a refreshing and not too glaring contrast with the white trims and cornice. The jointing employed is also uncommon, being seldon as much as one-quarter of an inch, struck with a fine line. The cement is a clean white in color, being made of white sand and pulverized sea-shells, which supplied oftentimes the lime for the mixture. When the brick was laid, the joint seems to have bulged slightly and then to have been carefully struck, making a clean straight line about one-sixteenth of an inch wide on the face of the bulge. The effect of this fine line on a narrow white joint gives an added crispness and refinement to the brickwork."

*Photograph: Harris & Ewing*

*The brick work of the Hyde House facade laid up in 1798 is a fine example of "tooled joint" work.*

The same workmanship is often found in the Georgetown Houses, for example, on the recently restored Patterson house, whose mortar-joints Mr. Waterman calls "hand-tooled." (See photograph on page 107.)

No glazed-end bricks have been used in Georgetown as they were in Williamsburg.

Under a coating of dirt and dust the bricks of these old houses have sometimes turned a chocolate-brown. If cleaned, however, they would undoubtedly reveal the original warm, pinky salmon color that seems to be characteristic of the locality.

In the letters of Gouverneur Morris and of Secretary Wolcott we have already seen references to the use of brick in the new city of Washington. The "History of the National Capital" by W. B. Bryan says; "As it was known that the clay in the vicinity was excellent for brick, by the first of October gangs of men were employed in getting out this material for building in the vicinity of the two public buildings, and later on kilns were erected there, where the brick used in these structures was made."

Daniel Carroll, one of the three Commissioners named by the President, made every exertion to provide accommodations for the First Congress in the Federal City, erecting numerous buildings on Capitol Hill and also furnishing brick for these houses, "as he was one of the largest brick-makers of that day." [7]

Brickyards and rubbish—an ever-present element of ugliness—surrounded the President's House. Dolly Madison complained that this was all she could see from her windows!

It is not generally known that a brick plant had to be moved to make place for the Penta-

[6] See "Brick Architecture of the Colonial Period in Maryland and Virginia."
[7] "Greenleaf and Law in the Federal City" by Allen C. Clark.

gon Building when it was erected. The plant was not abandoned but, re-established on a new site provided by the Government and on the same clay deposit, is still operating today.

*   *   *   *   *   *

For many years after the establishment of "the permanent Capital," there were grumblings and complaints about it. A bill was even introduced into Congress eight years later, urging reconsideration of the site and presenting valid reasons for removing the seat of Government to Philadelphia!

Fortunately the original plan was not abandoned. Our present magnificent Washington has developed from the genius of Major L'Enfant, and from the far-sightedness of our first President, who insisted that "the public buildings must look far beyond the needs of today."

What a distinguished group of gifted architects and designers was gathered together in one spot at that time! You will find much about them in the following pages—James Hoban, William Thornton, Benjamin Henry Latrobe, Thomas Jefferson, Stephen Hallet and, a little later, Charles Bulfinch of Boston. In one way or another each one of them has left his hall-mark on private dwellings in Washington and Georgetown, as well as on public buildings.

As Washington grew, the parent city of Georgetown declined. In 1800 its population had about equaled that of the Capital; ten years later Washington had doubled in size and Georgetown decreased forty percent. In 1851 the question of annexing Georgetown to Washington was discussed, and the Georgetown Advocate published the following amusing article:

"Is it best to marry Widower Georgetown to Miss Maryland or to Lady Washington?

"Miss Maryland has been accustomed to high living. She has given soirées and parties frequently at her palace at Annapolis, and invited the surrounding country to feast on champagne and oysters, while old Georgetown has been accustomed to live upon Potomac herring and corn bread, and by his economy has laid up a little property; which he is now going to throw away upon his extravagant lady-love Maryland. . . .

"Now, would it be well to marry Widower Georgetown to such an extravagant lady as this? The best we can do is to unite Georgetown to Washington. Lady Washington is little in debt compared to Miss Maryland, and she has an uncle, called Uncle Sam, who is very liberal towards her. He has a large revenue of fifty millions. . . .

"Now, as old Georgetown is rather poor, and hard pushed for money to get along, would it not be well to marry him to Lady Washington, so that he can share in her prosperity and wealth?"

Lady Washington won. Georgetown's charter as a city was revoked in 1871 and the area was incorporated into the District of Columbia, the streets being later joined with letters and numbers that continued those of Washington.[8]

It is still a regret among people who love the historic atmosphere of Georgetown and who wish to keep it intact that the charming old names like "Duck Lane" and "Gay Street," as well as the names of Jefferson, Madison, Monroe, Lafayette and Stoddert Streets, and the names of our Generals Greene, Montgomery and Washington, have all been discarded in favor of the Washington system, which is perhaps practical but certainly not poetic.

Far more serious than the loss of the old names, however, is the fact that many buildings recorded by the Historic American Building Survey have been destroyed. Under present conditions many others may disappear.

From a report to the Secretary of the Interior on the Preservation of Historic Sites and Buildings by J. Thomas Schneider in 1935, we learn that "there is no existing authority by which the National Park Service or any other Federal Agency can take appropriate steps to

[8] From "Origin and Government of the District of Columbia" by William Tindall.

prohibit or prevent the threatened destruction of a building not in Federal ownership which possesses historic interest, nor means by which the Federal Government can effectively cooperate with States, Private organizations and individuals toward such an end."

In Boston there is the Society for the Preservation of New England Antiquities, which has saved many beautiful old houses from destruction. In New York there is the Historical Society. The Colonial Dames, the D.A.R. and the Garden Clubs have all exerted their efforts to preserve historic spots in various parts of the country. And there are many other organizations with the same interest in safeguarding our national heritage. Is it not possible to link together the Presidents of all these separate groups, to include with them the heads of the large museums, and so to form a great National Association which could operate like the *National Monuments Commission in England* or the *Commission des Monuments in France?* Surely proper legislation could be obtained by such a group which would give it the power to protect and care for places connected with the history of this country and to preserve them for future generations.

*   *   *   *   *   *

The three men who have created this book on "Georgetown Houses" are now in Washington, in the service of the nation. In the past two years they have been able to devote only their hard-won leisure moments to accomplish this project, which has become an absorbing interest to each one of them.

Deering Davis, a member of this Institute, conceived the idea, persuaded the others to help, did the research, supervised the photography and compilation and arranged for the publication of the book.

Commander Ralph Cole Hall, USNR, contemporary St. Louis architect acted in the capacity of architectural advisor in the project.

Stephen P. Dorsey, descendant of the Dorsey and other distinguished Maryland families, a keen student of architecture and a writer of historical manuscripts, is responsible for the charming and readable text.

In conclusion, the authors wish me, first of all, to thank the owners of the houses shown for the gracious permission to photograph their homes. They also wish to extend their most sincere thanks to Miss Virginia Daiker of the Art Department, and Mrs. Clara E. LeGear of the Map Department, Library of Congress; Miss Mercedes Jordan, Chief of the Washingtonia Room, K Street Public Library; Miss Eva Nelson Gilbert of the Peabody Room, Georgetown Public Library; Dr. Herman Kahn, Chief of the Interior Archives; Mrs. Walter G. Peter, authoress and authority on Georgetown; Lieutenant Commander Charles E. Peterson, U.S.N.R., President of the Thornton Society of Washington; The National Society of Colonial Dames of America in the District of Columbia; Mr. Robert E. Lammond, Jr., of the Columbia and Real Estate Title Insurance Companies; Mr. Rex Curtiss of Harris and Ewing, and the Office of General U. S. Grant III for their many courtesies.

Nancy V. McClelland,<br/>A.I.D.

# TABLE OF CONTENTS

# LIST OF ILLUSTRATIONS

# THE HISTORICAL BACKGROUND

GEORGETOWN—once in Maryland—now part of the District of Columbia—scene of many important historical events—was founded three years after nearby Alexandria. By the latter part of the Eighteenth Century each had become a thriving port, daring to hope that it would eventually compare with New York or Philadelphia.

The locality, originally the site of the Indian village of Tahoga, was visited as early as 1608 by Captain John Smith. About 1703, it caught the fancy of a sturdy Scot, Colonel Ninian Beall, Commander in Chief of the Provincial Forces of Maryland, who in 1699 had been rewarded by an "Act of Gratuity" passed by the Assembly in recognition of his services "Upon all incursions and disturbances of neighboring Indians." Beall Patented 795 acres here and, probably thinking of the great Rock of Dunbarton, above the Firth of Clyde, near Glasgow, he gave that name to his new holding. In 1734 George Gordon became the owner of "Gordon's Rock Creek Plantation" of 300 acres next to Beall and since the majority of those who followed the first settlers were Scots, the area came to be called New Scotland Hundred. Pleasantly situated at the head of navigation, the land was a natural site for an urban center and the development of the surrounding region inevitably resulted in the establishment of the town itself.

On June 8, 1751, the Assembly of the Province of Maryland appointed six Commissioners whose survey was completed in February of the following year. "Knaves Disappointment," owned by George Gordon, as well as "Bealls Levels," and the "Rock of Dumbarton," owned by George Beall, son of the original settler, were the tracts found "most convenient" for the new center which was named for George II, the reigning king. Each owner was offered two town lots plus the price of condemnation. Gordon accepted, and Beall, after refusing to recognize the proceedings, finally agreed, with the declaration, however, that "I do hereby protest and declare that my acceptance of the said lots, which is by force, shall not debar me from future redress from the Commissioners or others, if I can have the rights of a British subject. God save the King." Two hundred and eighty pounds were paid for the sixty acres of townsite extending from the river about to the present N Street and from the site of Georgetown University approximately to 30th Street. The boundary stone marking the town's northeast corner still stands in the garden at 3014 N Street. The new town flourished as a port and tobacco inspection point. Its original eighty lots were supplemented by six further additions, but it was not until 1789 that it was formally incorporated.

The province had been founded at St. Mary's in 1634 by Leonard Calvert for his brother Cecil, second Lord Baltimore, and from that point settlement rapidly spread northward up Chesapeake Bay and the Potomac. Under the manorial system land grants were large, often consisting of thousands of acres, and through the unique feudal system established by the Lord Proprietor, many of the great planters became manorial lords, with rights of court baron and court leet over their tenants.

By the beginning of the Eighteenth Century most of the Potomac tidewater region had been taken up by aristocratic Maryland and Virginia families, but due to the size of the plantations, and the distances between neighbors settlements were sparse and many of the planters spent much time in the saddle. Their hospitality was abundant. Indeed, George Washington wrote that his family had not sat down alone to dinner in twenty years. Horse races, hunt meets and card parties were frequent, and except at "public times" in the provincial capitals when the courts and assembles were held with their attendant races, slave auctions, cock fights and theatricals, it was not until late in the colonial period that life centering about the great manors became gradually directed to the urban centers. Obviously the great planters were not the sole residents of these colonies. Certainly the largest segment of the population was made up of negro slaves upon whose labor the plantation economy was based. There were, too, very considerable numbers of white mechanics, artisans and laborers—the "little people"—most of whom had arrived as indentured servants who had bound themselves to their masters for five years of service in payment for their voyage to the new world. Then there were the small farmers who worked the less fertile tobacco lands themselves, perhaps with the help of a slave or two. It was difficult for this group to consign its product profitably to the English agents and gradually the larger planters became traders, buying the tobacco of their smaller competitors to whom they sold a variety of necessary goods and stores.

Out of this transition grew the need for Georgetown, laid out, as it was, at a natural place for an inspection and shipping point at the end of the "rolling" roads over which the great tobacco casks were rolled from the plantations, and where the western channel of the Potomac beyond Analostan Island offered water deep enough for large sailing ships. Already in 1755 General Braddock was able to write back to England that "never have I attended a more complete banquet, or met better dressed or better mannered people than I met on my arrival in George Town, which is named after his gracious Majesty." Men from the old plantation families and from the mother country saw promise in the place and they were joined by a substantial number of New England merchants. The warehouses grew, and by 1791 Washington himself described the town as "the greatest tobacco market in Maryland if not in the Union."

During the last quarter of the Eighteenth and the first quarter of the Nineteenth centuries, this busy seaport saw its ships carrying tobacco, flour, lumber and fish to its sister colonies, to the West Indies and abroad, and returning with sugar, spices, molasses, textiles, furniture and supplies of all sorts. Here too, by 1800 were a rope walk, a paper factory, a textile mill, numerous counting houses, shops and stores. Guns made at Henry Foxall's foundry during the war of 1812 contributed to Perry's victory on Lake Erie. Newspapers were published and banks were opened. The Great Conestoga wagons that rumbled through the streets carried Georgetown's products overland, and the new Potomac (later Chesapeake and Ohio) Canal was organized to open a water route to the west.

It has been said that "Colonial Williamsburg occupied during colonial times an area of about one mile square; had approximately 300 houses and a resident population of about 3,000 which increased to 7,000 during "public times." Of these colonial buildings sixty-six have been repaired or restored, while 84 have been reproduced on colonial foundations. During the first twenty years of the Nineteenth Century Georgetown also occupied about one square mile but according to census records had a resident population of 5,000 to 7,000. By the same ratio of dwellings to population as at Williamsburg, Georgetown probably consisted at that time of about 700 buildings of which 400 are estimated to have been of brick and 300 of wooden construction. Of these buildings 300 were probably brick dwellings of the type shown in this book, with the balance made up of stores, warehouses, schools, churches, etc. Today 200 structures of this period remain, or over 25%, a remarkable tribute to the builders of the day. The streets on which they stood, since alphabetized and numbered, bore such delightful names as Cherry, Duck, and Fishing Lanes, Gay, High, Water, Back, and Bridge Streets, and simply Wapping, Causeway and Keys. The modern system, although perhaps more practical, is certainly less pleasant, and there are those inhabitants who still resent it.

Early Georgetown was the site of a number of schools, and here in 1789 Georgetown College was founded by Bishop John Carroll. The town was frequently visited by theatrical companies, and it abounded in dancing and drawing masters. Here about 1803 Gilbert Stuart spent two years painting the portraits of the great of the town and of the new capital city adjacent to it. The Anchor, The Sailors, The Sign of the Indian King and other inns were vigorous centers of life. The Fountain Inn, also called Suter's Tavern, was the scene of many of the transactions in connection with the establishment of the Federal City across Rock Creek, and here the disputed presidential election was decided by the House of Representatives in favor of Thomas Jefferson rather than John Adams, his Federalist opponent. The great Union Tavern, later Crawford's Hotel, built in 1796, became famous for its Pompeian ballroom, its gentlemen's arched corridor or colonnade opening on the courtyard, and its stables for fifty horses. A large coach, The Royal George, took legislator guests to the Capitol and back. Here at various times stayed Louis Philippe, Jerome Bonaparte, Talleyrand, John Adams, Washington Irving, Robert Fulton and many other famous personages. Here the night before his duel with Henry Clay, John Randolph of Roanoke played whist and quoted poetry while his will was amended. Jefferson lived here for a time while he was Secretary of State. Here Francis Scott Key lived for twenty years as a lawyer and District Attorney and from his house on Bridge Street left for his rendezvous aboard a British man of war lying below Fort McHenry and the creation of the verses that epitomize love of country for all Americans everywhere. The town was visited at one time or another during the Early Federal Period by practically all of the great and near great who passed through the capital city painfully coming into existence on the other side of the creek. Washington, in his journeys north from Mount Vernon, was a frequent visitor to the town where he had both family connections and business interests. He was one of the founders of the Potomac Company to promote a canal westward to the Ohio and it was in Georgetown that he organized the survey and purchase of the land for the new Federal Capital. On such visits he frequently stopped with the family of Mr. Thomas Peter. He dined at Wise's Tavern enroute to New York to his inauguration as first President of the United States, and The *Pennsylvania Packet* of May 5th, stated:

> "George-Town, April 23.—Last Thursday, passed through this town, on his way to New-York, the Most Illustrious the President of the United States of America, with Charles Thomson, Esq.; Secretary to Congress. His Excellency arrived at about 2 o'clock, on the banks of the Potowmack, escorted by a respectable corps of gentlemen from Alexandria, where the George-Town ferry boats, properly equipped, received his Excellency and suite, and safely landed them under the acclamations of a large crowd of their grateful fellow-citizens—who beheld their Fabius in the evening of his days, bid adieu to the peaceful retreat of Mount Vernon, in order to save his country once more, from confusion and anarchy. From this place his Excellency was escorted by a corps of gentlemen, commanded by Col. William Deakins, Jun. to Mr. Spurrier's Tavern, where the escort from Baltimore take charge of him."

During the following eight years which kept him from residence at Mount Vernon, he crossed Maryland on visits to his home on an average of twice a year, making the sixteen trips, by fast coach almost continually enveloped in the clouds of dust kicked up by his mounted escorts.

After seven years of bitter conflict between North and South over the location of the Federal City, the Residence Bill was passed in July 1790 and under it the following October President Washington assumed his role as agent for Congress to choose the site for a permanent seat of government, to acquire the lands and to appoint building commissioners. In January 1791 the Potomac site east of Georgetown was selected, and happily against almost universal opposition the President supported the plan of the French military engineer, Pierre Charles l'Enfant, sufficiently strongly to secure its adoption. Today it is considered America's foremost achievement in municipal planning. Inevitably the human desire to secure the best locations in the new city, actually still only in the planning stage, resulted in a veritable tempest of speculation though it was not until June 1800 that the seat of government was removed from Philadelphia and established in its permanent location in Washington. Building of the new Federal City did not at once affect the commercial development of its neighbor. In fact, for the first decade of the nineteenth century the older sister in many ways overshadowed the sprawling infant, and continued to be the home of many of the foreign envoys who gave it a certain world consciousness and cosmopolitanism in addition to the quieter and more established culture that comes with greater age. In August 1814 all of the public buildings in the new city, with the exception of the Post and Patent Office, were burned by British forces under General Ross and Admiral Cockburn. Although very little private property was destroyed and the public buildings were rebuilt in three years, the shabbiness of Washington was in decided contrast to older Georgetown.

As late as 1835 a British visitor, Harriet Martineau, wrote:

"The city itself is unlike any other that ever was seen, straggling out hither and thither, with a small house or two a quarter of a mile from any other; so that making calls 'in the city' we had to cross ditches and stiles, and walk alternately on grass and pavements, and strike across a field to reach a street—Then there was the society, singularly compounded from the most varied of elements; foreign ambassadors, the American government, members of Congress, from Clay and Webster down to Davy Crockett, Burton from Missouri; and Cuthbert; with the freshest Irish brogue, from Georgia; flippant young belles, 'pious' wives dutifully attending their husbands, and groaning over the frivolities of the place; grave judges, saucy travellers, pert newspaper reporters, melancholy Indian Chiefs and timid New England ladies, trembling on the verge of the vortex."

Although certainly less beautiful, this earlier Washington sounds not unlike descriptions of the wartime city we know today. Nor was it greatly improved physically by 1862 when Mary Clemmer Ames described it:

"Capitol Hill, dreary, desolate and dirty stretched away into an uninhabited desert,—arid hill and sodden plain showed alike the horrid trail of war. Forts bristled above every hill-top.—Shed hospitals covered acres in every suburb.—the rattle of the anguish-laden ambulance, the piercing cries of the sufferers whom it carried, made morning, noon and night too dreadful to be borne." while "The streets were filled with—new regiments,—their banners all untarnished as they marched up Pennsylvania Avenue, playing 'The girl I left behind me.'"

This was the new Washington under siege, the Washington that for four years was an Army headquarters. During the preceding quarter century, Georgetown's importance as a commercial port, industrial center and canal terminus had gradually gone into eclipse with the advent of the railroads. It was natural that, during this period of growing conflict of opinion between North and South, the sympathy of a great many of its people should lie with the South—the land of their origin—and their blue cockades were worn openly in the same streets that were later to be hung with black after Lincoln's assassination and to witness Southern girls crossing to the other side rather than pass under the National colors hanging over the doors of the Union hospitals located in the town.

With the flamboyance and excitement of the reconstruction years that followed the war, however, came a physical regeneration that transformed Washington from the shabby village that it had been to something like the present metropolis. It was natural that Georgetown, many of whose residents had lost their wealth in Washington real estate speculation, should become principally a residential section while the warehouses crumbled along its once busy water front. Indeed its face became considerably altered by new rows of ugly Victorian dwellings, many of which remain. In 1871 it relinquished the separate charter which it had kept even after its inclusion within the District of Columbia, and by Act of Congress became a part of Washington. Georgetown's golden age became a memory, and the principal glory of the community became the lovely relics of its past.

Still the quiet suburb has retained a unique self-entity within the great capital that now entirely surrounds it. The elements of other days remain in a personality that has caused it to be described poetically as a beautiful old dogwood, always in flower, standing beside the oak in its prime which is Washington proper.

17

# FEDERAL ARCHITECTURE OF GEORGETOWN, D. C.

GEORGETOWN, quiet suburb of the Nation's Capital, is in itself a living record of the Republic's architecture since its founding. Federal, Classic Revival, Victorian and Modern homes —all are here, but the architectural significance and the greatest charm of the town lie in those structures built during the first fifty years of the Nation's existence. These homes have seen many wars come and go, and to them the confusion of the Capital in a time of emergency is nothing new. Through Georgetown passed part of Braddock's forces on their fateful way to defeat at Duquesne in 1755. From Georgetown, men, ships, supplies went forth in the cause of the thirteen colonies, and here Washington, victorious, directed the planning of the new Federal Capital to bear his name. From its heights, Georgetown's residents watched the fires in 1814. In the sixties they knew the legion of the wounded and the feel of a beleaguered city, and they opened their doors to the war workers who packed the city of 1917.

Overshadowed by the city she had helped to build, Georgetown fell into neglect late in the last century. In recent years, however, government officials, officers of the services, newspapermen and others have restored many of the smaller houses whose charm was obvious even under their cloak of neglect, and other more enterprising restorations have contributed to the re-establishment of a proper setting for a brilliant social life similar to that for which Georgetown once was famous. Uniquely too, this living "town within a city" retains its individuality, its entity, and its pride in its tradition. Here one feels the qualities of a small, very charming and very old town, and in these qualities is its architectural significance.

Fiske Kimball has said in his "Regional Types in Early American Architecture" that "in the South it is only at Charleston that we find really urban types. Even at Annapolis the houses are semi-rural." However, in Georgetown, developed principally in the half-century from 1775 to 1825 there does exist an urban type of dwelling with a distinct local idiom adapted to the lives of its builders and to local climate and materials.

From a glance at Georgetown houses of the type which flourished during the town's "golden age" it is evident that they are not "Colonial" in the literal sense of the word. Rather they are true examples of the Federal tradition, influenced by Colonial antecedents, but built during the early days of the new Republic—examples of a school which flourished under the patronage of Thomas Jefferson who, as Secretary of State under Washington and as President, had very considerable influence in fostering America's Federal style. Here the Colonial style of Georgian derivation gave way to a transitional one of greater Classic feeling which became our first national architectural expression.

In reflecting, it may be conjectured that the transition from the Colonial of Georgian derivation consciously paralleled the interest of the new republic in its prototypes, the Greek and Roman Republics. Washington himself, as we shall see, was an enthusiastic patron of the Federal style with an interest in architecture more profound than he himself realized— a fact made obscure by the Colonial features of most of Mount Vernon, and the preoccupation with them of the public mind.

The homes of the period possess a delicacy of scale which distinguishes them, and which was the result of a masterful adaptation of elements of Classic precedent, reduced from the scale of stone to that for work in wood. The brickwork is most frequently of Flemish bond, expertly laid up in large-size bricks, sand-moulded by hand, and now turned a beautiful shade between cherry and chocolate color. Corbeled courses frequently form the eave ornament beneath a simple gutter. Almost without exception these houses are of the simple gabled type, with the roof pitch becoming less acute toward the end of the first quarter of the nineteenth century. The larger houses frequently have chimneys in pairs at the roof-ends flush with the walls, and a flat deck between, with sloping roofs to the front and rear. Dormers are gabled, often with a circular-head upper sash with ingenious arrangements of muntins separating small panes. Muntins, mouldings and vertical treatment of the dormers with pilasters or colonettes were beautifully contrived, and a similarity exists which suggests the work of the same draftsmen or millwrights.

The fenestration is thoughtfully arranged, and in the earlier examples consisted of windows in the first storey having six panes in the lower sash and nine panes above, while the second storey windows were, typically, twelve-light openings. While a simplicity exists in the surrounding mouldings, an ingenious variation occurs which is evidence of a scholarly application to detail. Frequent use of delicate wrought iron work in handrails foreshadows the early Victorian popularity of this decorative medium in Georgetown and is, in certain cases, reminiscent of New Orleans, although it is of a simpler type than the fine ornamental examples in the South.

The larger houses carry porticoes of good proportion and moderate size. Examples are to be found in Tudor Place and Dumbarton House (illustrated on pages 89 to 103). Neither of these houses is characteristic of the Georgetown urban type. They are instead manorial in character, each with a large central mass flanked by wings which were added at a different time. However, they constitute excellent examples of the work of Thornton and Latrobe. Occasionally a balustrade was used over the porch, as at Mackall Square, and there was excellent application of recessed panels beneath windows—sometimes ornamented by cast lead swags as in Cox's Row—and of recessed blind arches where the monumental scale permitted. A consistency of restraint and simplicity prevail in these structures which remind one of the general "quality" evident in the life and effort of the new Republic.

Outside trim is of a simple type using classic mouldings and is delicate in scale. Sills and lintels are typically of stone, frequently with a finely moulded key block or with raised, square corner blocks bearing an indented circular ornament. Doorways are found with circular or eliptical heads, and often with sidelights separated from the door opening by finely reeded or moulded mullions. A few examples remain of leaded glass transoms which are rich and beautiful in their design. Shutters and entrance door were invariably painted dark green with all other wood trim white.

Four basic types of Georgetown houses stand as a document of the time: the manorial type flanked by lower wings which occupy generous plots of ground, the larger ell-shaped house having a two storey wing for servants extending back through the near garden, the small urban dwelling of either rectangular or ell-shape which is the principal subject of this book, and lastly, the small New England type of frame house. The typical, small houses are the most often illustrated in the following plates although some examples of others are included. Frequently they are of the English basement type, and entrance to the main living floor is by steps from the sidewalk, sometimes curved, and built of stone or of brick with stone treads having a "bull-nose" moulding around the front and ends. Others are entered directly from the sidewalk and have one step to gain the level of the floor.

The entrance and hall are at the side, the hallway having two or three living rooms opening from it, and at the rear, access to the ell or servants' wing, should the house have one. Such wings were built either at the time of the erection of the main house or as later additions were required by growing families. The kitchens were located in the wings or in the half-basements, with the dining room adjacent to it or on the floor above as may have suited the tastes of the occupant. This type of dwelling was built abutting directly on the street, which at the time was usually unpaved and through which cattle, pigs and turkeys were often driven to market. To the rear one finds lovely secluded gardens, often with fine boxwood or magnolias, and occasionally an original shed or smokehouse. These dependencies were

19

most often of brick and so placed as to be both accessible and artistically pleasant. Overlooking the gardens, frequently one sees pillared galleries opening on each floor from the hallway or from individual rooms,—admirably adapted to the hot summer climate. The owner of this type of house lived at the rear, on the garden side, as we might well do today when automobile traffic crowds the streets.

The photographs which follow have generally been restricted to the original Federal portion of each house, since some have been supplemented by later additions. It may be noted that, in certain instances, the level of the street has been lowered and consequently the consideration of the mass and scale must be from the standpoint of its original location and placement.

The interiors of these Georgetown houses hold even more of interest to the present day architect, interior decorator or house-owner than do their exteriors. Houses of similar medium size maintained very much the same outward appearance for the 150 years from 1680 to 1830, but their interiors, both as to architectural detail and decorative furnishings, had several clearly defined epochs. There are excellent examples of the artistic accomplishments of these early builders in the houses treated in the following photographs. The wood paneling, carving, and heavier wood trim of the preceding eras were completely set aside. Delicately moulded architraves and dadoes were much in evidence and mantels with gesso or cast ornaments in the form of eagles, swags and decorated bands were employed. Arched openings appear frequently in the hall-way and many have reveals cleverly reeded or panelled, and moulded key and impost blocks. Details were generally of classic derivation, used with great restraint, and interiors were singularly free from the more elaborate tendencies of the Brothers Adam.

Plaster from ceiling to base board was the rule. Often no chair rail and sometimes not even a ceiling cornice was employed. Wood trim around doors and windows many times turned back with a moulding from the reveal for less than two inches on the wall. (See page 108.) This moulding was of extreme delicacy and refinement with beautiful clean cut lines. The simple treatment of walls and openings gave an illusion of greater space in these medium size or small rooms, which were a perfect setting for the classic Sheraton, Phyfe, and Regency furniture of the time or acted as a foil for the Queen Anne, Hepplewhite or Chippendale pieces of former eras.

Walls were either painted or papered; stair balusters were straight-sided rectangles. Fabrics for drapery were small patterned chintz, toiles often depicting scenes of American life or history, silks and satins in classic designs. Floors were wide planked hard Georgia Pine oiled and waxed and were covered with rugs from China, Persia, France or England. Hardware, such as doorknobs, was brass; small in scale and very unpretentious. Locks were usually of the large brass or iron box type. Wall colors and trim were often white or cream. Almost as usual was Adam Green or light blue on walls, with white or cream wood trim. However, almost all colors and tones were used according to the owners taste.

The interior photographs which follow demonstrate the suitability of this simple late Georgian type to many styles and kinds of furniture either used together or kept relatively pure as to period. One may have the most costly and rare examples of the cabinet or chair-makers art; simple maple and cherry pieces of less intrinsic value or very inexpensive but appropriate painted pieces such as the Hitchcock chair, which was manufactured in the early 19th Century as the first truly American mass production furniture item. Nor are good Modern examples out of place; in fact, they seem to be enhanced by the superb functionalism of these Georgian interiors.

The scale is, as indicated above, expertly adapted to local building materials, and while the general mass and disposition of motifs shows the influence of the Georgian antecedents of the day, these houses are truly American.

# DR. WILLIAM THORNTON, 1761-1828
## Architect of the Federal Period

ARCHITECT, inventor, painter and horseracer, William Thornton was a large man of unusually handsome mien, who knew almost everything, who was genuinely interested in letting almost everyone know about it, who might have gained greater fame had he concentrated in one field of endeavor rather than on "architecture, philosophy, politics, finance, astronomy, medicine, botany, poetry, painting, religion, agriculture, in short all subjects by turns."

Born of Quaker parents May 27, 1761 on the tiny island of Jost Van Dyke in the West Indies, he was sent to England as a boy and received his preliminary education while living with indulgent aunts on the family estate, Green Air, in Lancaster. He entered the College of Edinburgh and took his doctor's degree in medicine in 1784. He then went to Paris to continue his studies and attached himself to the Countess de Beauhearnais, an aunt of the Empress Josephine's first husband. While in Paris, the young man who was already such an excellent penman that as a boy he had been able to fool his uncle with a £5 note of his own manufacture, studied drawing and painting with such talent that he created an excellent miniature of his new patroness.

In 1787 he landed in New York, then went to Wilmington and finally to Philadelphia, where his plans for the Library Company of Philadelphia won the competition for its proposed new building.* Thornton stated in a letter that this was his first architectural attempt and that he had never actually studied the subject until later, when he determined to submit a design for the National Capitol and studied "for a number of months night and day" while working on the drawings. However, from the tone of his letter it seems not unlikely that he was playing down his talents. It is more probable that he had been interested in architecture along with his other artistic researches in England and France, for he had been named a member of the Society of Antiquaries before he left Edinburgh.

In Philadelphia he became a member of the fashionable set, a friend of Dr. Franklin's, and at twenty-nine the husband of fifteen-year old Anna Maria Brodeau, talented and lovely daughter of a prominent Quaker family, who was later to study under Gilbert Stuart and acting as her husband's draughtsman, to make detailed drawings of his rough design sketches. After a two years' honeymoon in the West Indies, the newlyweds returned to Philadelphia in 1792, where Mrs. Brodeau had a pleasant house ready on Chestnut Street with some $2,200 worth of furnishings. Thornton had already begun his plans for the National Capitol while in the West Indies and received notice that his plan had won the competition in April, 1793. On September 18 of the same year the cornerstone was laid by President Washington, who, on the occasion, wore a Masonic apron embroidered by Madame Lafayette. Thornton at first declined to superintend erection of the building but came to Georgetown, living at 3221 M Street. However, several superintendents of construction were dismissed for attempting to alter his plan, and eventually its creator was placed in charge. He was appointed one of the District Commissioners and worked in close collaboration with the President and Major l'Enfant on the planning of the capital city. He sold his M Street house in 1797 and moved across Rock Creek to Washington where he maintained a city residence at 1331 F Street until his death in 1828.

Without doubt Thornton became the leader of the triumvirate of great architects of this area during that period. Of this group, James Hoban (1762-1831), who collaborated with

* Since razed. However, good photographs still exist.

21

*Dr. William Thornton*
By permission of the Columbia Historical
Society. Library of Congress photograph
A self portrait

Thornton during the early construction of the Capitol, is best known as architect of the White House or "President's Palace" as it was first known, which he designed in 1792. Unfortunately the present greatly enlarged building has lost much of the charm of the original simpler design and it can hardly be classed as domestic architecture. He planned the original State and Navy buildings which have since been destroyed (though the original drawings remain), as well as several hotels, but there are no known records of his planning domestic structures.

Thornton's principal rival, and the third member of the group, Benjamin H. Latrobe (1764-1820), who succeeded the doctor as Director of Works for the Capitol in 1803, is famous for his quarrels with Thornton over its design. He deserves lasting notice for his creation there of an American order of architecture through the use of cotton blossoms, tobacco leaves, and Indian corn in the columns and capitals of the great structure where they may still be seen. He was the architect of St. John's Church on Lafayette Square, and notable examples of his domestic designs remain in nearby Decatur House and in Dumbarton House in Georgetown, restored according to his plans of about 1809. While other local architects of the period are known, no definite examples of their work exist with the exception of the central portion of the building which houses the United States District Court of the District of Columbia—completed in 1820 as the City Hall from the plans of George Hadfield (1764-1826), an Englishman who had won many architectural prizes in London before coming to Washington to help in the erection of the Capitol.

In any case, it is in the field of domestic architecture that Thornton was by far the most influential local architect of the period. Substantiated documentary and physical evidence proves his designing a double house for Washington on Capitol Hill and one house each for Daniel Carroll, the great landowner, and his brother in the same area. Under the circumstances it is probable that he was also the architect for Carroll's Row, which once stood on the site of the present Library of Congress. Kimball attributes exquisite Homewood in Baltimore—one of Charles Carroll of Carrollton's great houses—to Thornton and we know from Mrs. Thornton's diary that he designed the residence of Thomas Law, wealthy and aristocratic English resident of Washington who married Eliza Parke Custis, granddaughter of Martha Washington. Law built several houses on Capitol Hill as well as some twenty in the Greenleaf Point area where he lost a fortune in an attempt to make it the fashionable residential section of the new city. Surely Thornton, who planned Law's personal residence, greatly influenced these other houses, if he did not actually design them.

There is little wonder that Fiske Kimball, in his foreword to the second volume of Great Georgian Houses, says that his influence in Maryland was so great that even today Baltimore architects feel that they must work sympathetically, or that Glenn Brown terms him the greatest architect of his time.

There is absolute proof that he planned Tudor Place in Georgetown for Thomas Peter and his wife, Martha Parke Custis, another of the three beautiful Custis girls, granddaughter of Mrs. Washington and sister of both Mrs. Thomas Law and Mrs. Lawrence Lewis.

The third Custis granddaughter, Washington's favorite, married his nephew, Lawrence Lewis, who built Woodlawn a portion of which still stands on that part of the original Mount Vernon tract, given the couple by the first President. There is every proof that here too Thornton was the designing architect of this exceptionally lovely structure.

Thornton was also the architect of St. Johns Church, Georgetown, as well as of Octagon House, the unusual and beautiful mansion near the White House, completed in 1800 for John Tayloe of Mount Airy, one of the most powerful and wealthy planters of Virginia. Tayloe was persuaded by his close friend General Washington to build his town house in the new city rather than in Philadelphia, as he had first intended. The house, supposed to be haunted by the ghost of the original owner's beautiful daughter who threw herself down the great stairwell as a result of her father's refusal to allow her to marry a young Englishman, was originally connected by secret underground passages with the White House and with the Potomac River. It has served as the executive mansion and it was here that President Madison signed the ratification of the Treaty of Ghent. Its selection in 1902 as the permanent home of the American Institute of Architects is full testimony to its perfection.

Thomas Jefferson, foremost exponent of the New Classic style of architecture, thought highly of William

*Mrs. William Thornton*
*By permission of the Columbia Historical Society. Library of Congress photograph*
Portrait by Dr. Thornton

Thornton and asked his friend for preliminary sketches for the University of Virginia, which were used in part. President Madison wrote, too, that Thornton was the architect for the main portion of his estate, Montpelier. With such powerful and fashionable patrons as Washington, Jefferson and Madison, it is hardly strange that seemingly half the houses in Georgetown are attributed to him, and that he exercised so great an influence on the architectural style of the whole District of Columbia. Without doubt, more than any other individual, he was the creator of the Federal type of house characteristic of the Georgetown section of the District, if not the "virtual creator of the Federal Style" as he has been called. Certainly he is the father of the type of urban house illustrated in the following pages as the best of its period, singularly suited to city living today.

A sketch of this amazing figure, however, would be incomplete if his other varied activities were not at least mentioned. He painted beautifully, still lifes and miniatures, and his excellent portraits of Washington, Jefferson, Dolly Madison, Mrs. Thornton as well as a self-portrait are still in existence. The first Patent Commissioner, he was an inventor in his own right, an extensive patent holder, and a close collaborator of both John Fitch and Robert Fulton in the development of the steam boat. He was a magistrate and, though a Quaker, a fearless and active captain of cavalry militia.

A member of the Medical Society of Edinburgh, he organized a fire insurance company and drew up a prospectus for a North Carolina Gold Mine Company and for a public market. He first proposed a Washington monument and advocated a Panama canal. A sheep breeder and horse lover, he built a race track in Washington. A poet, a novelist, a philosopher, he advocated eventual union of North and South America, the abolition of slavery, and establishment of a republic of freedmen in Africa, such as Liberia. Continuous candidate for a diplomatic mission to Latin America, he was an early advocate of the good neighbor policy.

Considered a dreamer by many in high places, this intimate of Washington, Jefferson, Adams, Madison and Monroe was nevertheless a factor in government because of his acquaintance with the powerful at home, his accord with the ministers from abroad and his correspondence with scientists the world over. How prophetic were the members of Congress who told him that he had lived a hundred years too soon, and the wife who wrote after his death "His views were too extended, his plans too vast to be embraced by men generally." Such a man was this old world son of the new Republic, who gave so much beauty to his country.

# THE WALKER HOUSE
## C. 1805
## 2806 N Street, N. W.

The history of this house—probably built about 1805—is as incomplete as its interior detail is lovely. Thomas Beall sold the property in 1804 to John M. Gannt. The title records for the intermediate period are lost, but it was purchased from Elisha Williams by Thomas Robertson in 1810, and resold to Thomas Clarke in 1811. It then became the property of Thomas Corcoran, originally of Limerick, who had come to Georgetown in 1788 after five years in Baltimore. However, the prosperous leather merchant, mayor, magistrate and postmaster, who died in 1830, lived for many years in the house which he had built at 3119 M Street in 1791.

The house has been beautifully and intelligently restored by its present owners, Mr. and Mrs. John Walker, 3rd.

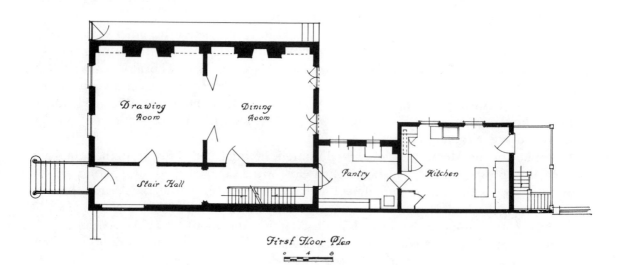

First Floor Plan

*Photograph : Harris & Ewing*

The new appearance of the facade was caused by the necessity of sand blasting to remove many coats of paint. Note the multiplicity of detail on the dormers.

*Photograph: Harris & Ewing*

Simplicity of scale can be most effective as shown by these mouldings and the stone overdoor

The garden is typical and very lovely

*Photograph : Harris & Ewing*

The entrance hall. An interior arch of equisite design complements the front overdoor

Vista of the living room. The original opening between "parlors" has been greatly enlarged to make them one room. A corresponding fireplace and bookcases are not shown.

# THE JOHN STODDERT HAW HOUSE
## C. 1812
## 2808 N Street, N. W.

Little is known of this fine example of the Federal town house except that it was built by John Stoddert Haw, nephew of Benjamin Stoddert, one of the founders of Christ Church, Georgetown, probably in the first decade of the Nineteenth Century. It was purchased by the late Admiral and Mrs. Spencer Wood who were among the first to begin the restoration of this section of the town. The garden is lovely and the interior of the house is unusual in its freedom from the Victorian alterations that have marred many other superb buildings of the period.

*Photograph: Harris & Ewing*

An example of simple dignity achieved in a house of moderate size

31

*Photograph: Harris & Ewing*

A true interpretation of the Federal feeling. Lintels and sills are of painted wood—a common practice in 1800—giving an attractive, fresh, yet soft appearance. The worn stone shows that even the stair treads are original.

The branches of fine old trees protect this sylvan garden at the rear—a perfect setting for *al fresco* dining.

*Photograph: Stewart Bros.*

A particularly fine interior arch and fan light occupy the entrance hall

An exquisite classic mantel

# THE DECATUR HOUSE
## C. 1779
## 2812 N Street, N. W.

This house has persistently been associated with the name of Decatur although no authentic sources for the legend are known. It is said to have been erected in 1779 and is known to have been the home of Judge Morsell at one time. According to tradition, Mrs. Susan Wheeler Decatur came here to live after the death of the Commodore in his duel with Captain James Barron at Bladensburgh March 22, 1820. Decatur House on Lafayette Square, built by Decatur for his bride according to Latrobe's plans in 1819, shortly after the tragedy was leased to the Russian Minister by the young widow. She then came to Georgetown where she lived until her death in 1860.

Seven years after her husband's death, Mrs. Decatur, still dwelling upon her personal tragedy, refused to enter Washington proper lest she meet his opponent, or his second, whom she considered much to blame. As a result, in the words of an English visitor of that time, "She sees a great deal of company at home." Certainly the walls of her home sheltered many of the great of other days; Mr. W. W. Corcoran, later the philanthropist; General Van Rensselaer, the New York patron; Mexican Prince Iturbide and his American wife, and many other distinguished persons were her frequent guests.

Later, Mrs. Decatur, who had become a devout Catholic, probably through her close friendship with the Carroll family, moved to a frame house near Georgetown College. Her grave is in the cemetery there, and several mementoes of the Commodore may be seen today at the University. This house, well known for its fine doorway, is the property of Mr. and Mrs. Franklin Mott Gunther and has been leased by the Countess de Martino.

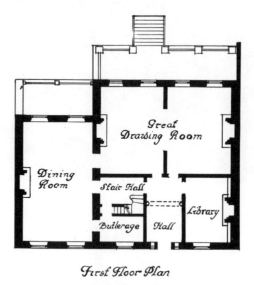

First Floor Plan

Scale of Feet

36

A superb example of function and form

*Photograph: Harris & Ewing*

Its hospitable entrance shows carefully worked-out detail. Note graceful stone arch and original iron work. The fan light and stone overdoor are very fine.

Formerly one room in width, this narrow house was joined to its larger neighbor by the simple expedient of knocking out a wall.

*Photograph : Harris & Ewing*

This charming room occupies the whole first floor of the little house shown on the preceding page. A fine old pine mantel is used and the carved cornice and chair rail are closely related.

*Photograph: Harris & Ewing*

Here one large and handsome living room has been made from two. A similar old mantel is at the opposite end; the bookcases are attractive recent additions. The floor plan is unusual as the living room runs across the house. Note fine example of window moulding indicative of the period.

The south gallery, almost hidden by the trees—a characteristic feature of Georgetown houses. From it one has a view of the garden, and beyond the housetops a magnificent sweep of the Potomac.

The garden as seen from the gallery

# THE FOXALL HOUSE
## C. 1790
## 2908 N Street, N. W.

The detail and proportion of this simple little house are intimate and charming. Built in the Eighteenth Century it was once owned as an investment by Henry Foxall, at whose foundry guns were made for the American Forces in 1812. Mr. Foxall, Mayor of the town in 1819, and a convert to Methodism, was known for his strict enforcement of the old "blue laws" against profaning the sabbath and for his practice of buying slaves whom he set free after they had learned a trade.

When the British entered the Capital in 1814 the Foxall foundry was one of the military objectives marked for destruction. Henry Foxall vowed that he would build a church if God would spare his property. The expeditionary force was turned back by a furious hurricane, and Foundry Methodist Church in Washington, the fulfillment of his vow, is the church at which Prime Minister Churchill worshipped with President Roosevelt on the occasion of their meeting in Washington in 1943!

The little house formerly was covered with white plaster. It has now been enclosed within a tall brick wall and is used by Mr. and Mrs. Robert J. Randolph, the owners, as one house in conjunction with the fine replica of a Federal house next door.

*Photograph: Harris & Ewing*

A high wall plays an imposing role in the restoration of this modest house

*Photograph: Harris & Ewing*

Wrought iron entrance gate—a happy choice

The small house grew by this new addition at the side. The stone lintel, rail and steps are old.

# THE LAIRD-DUNLOP HOUSE
## C. 1799
## 3014 N Street, N. W.

The central portion of this imposing brick mansion was built about 1799 by John Laird, the prosperous owner of one of early Georgetown's great tobacco warehouses. During its construction, he rented Thomas Beall's large house across the street. It is not unlikely that this house was designed by Thornton because of its unusual arched first story windows, which are identical to those of Thomas Law's house on Greenleaf Point, Washington, attributed with reasonable certainty to the great architect.

The house was inherited by John Laird's daughter Margaret in 1833. She lived there with her aunt, Elizabeth Dick, another spinster, for many years devoting much of her time to the Presbyterian Church and the Orphan Asylum. On her death the house passed to her sister, Barbara, (Mrs. James Dunlop) and became known thereafter as the Dunlop house.

Judge Dunlop was at various times Secretary of the Corporation of Georgetown, a law partner of Francis Scott Key, and Chief Justice of the Supreme Court of the District of Columbia until he was removed from the latter office as a southern sympathizer by President Lincoln. His son, William Laird Dunlop, who lived here for a number of years, always kept his own cow and killed his own hogs each fall. The old smoke house remains just east of the house and one of the original town boundary markers still stands in the large garden.

In 1915 the mansion was purchased from William Laird Dunlop's heirs by Robert Todd Lincoln, eldest son of the President, one time Secretary of War and Ambassador to England. His widow lived there until the house was sold to Mrs. Arthur Woods, a granddaughter of J. Pierpont Morgan I, and a direct descendant of Alexander Hamilton. Extensive wings have been added to the original house which today serves as a fitting setting for her beautiful furniture, portraits and tapestries.

*Photograph: Harris & Ewing*

There are numerous later additions but this shows the original facade with its imposing entrance. To the left a glimpse of later additions. The fan light carries out the exact semicircle of the heads of the first story windows.

# THE RIGGS-RILEY HOUSE
## C. 1805
## 3038 N Street, N. W.

The fine town house of typical smaller "Georgetown" type known to Georgetown citizens for so many years as "old Doctor Riley's" was probably built about 1805. In any case, it was sold on March 24, 1812 by James S. Marshall to William S. Nicholls and Romulus Riggs. The latter, who was born in Brookeville, Montgomery County, Maryland, and who had married a Miss Dorsey in 1810, sometime before 1835 moved to Philadelphia where he became known as an influential and well-to-do merchant. An authority on Georgetown history believes that he lived in this house for some years before he sold it to Dr. Joshua Riley.

A number of medical students received their basic medical training in Dr. Riley's small one story brick office to the east of the house, much as young men once "read law" in the office of an established attorney. Among them were Dr. Armistead Peter, later of Tudor Place, and Waldemer and Boris Bodisco, nephews of the famed Russian Minister. Mrs. Riley's niece, Juliet Murray, was married to John Marbury, Jr., in this house in 1851, and the daughter of the house, Miss Marianna Riley, lived here with her sister-in-law for years after the Doctor's death.

Upon Miss Riley's death the house was sold and resold a number of times, until it became the property of Colonel (U.S. Marine Corps) and Mrs. Henry Leonard. The old office was razed to make way for a large service wing, but the garden and the house itself have been restored to the quaint beauty of their earliest days.

One of its beauties is its almost perfect scale—shown clearly in this view of the street facade

*Photograph : Harris & Ewing*

The detail and thoughtful scale of these dormers force great respect for their designers.  In some as many as seventeen hand-carved mouldings are used.

Entrance—Note delicate detail in overdoor

*Photograph : Harris & Ewing*

An original interior arch and stair for which no words of praise are necessary

A beautiful bedroom with mantel and furniture original

Judging from the exterior facade, it would be difficult to realize that so important and beautiful a garden joined the rear gallery.

The superb planning and great size are even more evident here

# THE COLONEL JOHN COX HOUSE
## C. 1805
## 3339 N Street, N. W.

Probably the finest examples of the Federal "row" house standing in Georgetown are those built by Colonel John Cox, about 1805, at the corner of N and 34th Streets. They are large, of ell shape, and are distinguished by their exquisitely fine dormers and leaden swags in the recessed panels which relieve the severity of the facade. They are unique in standing back some distance from the street, which affords them sizable door yards at the sacrifice of the gardens at the rear.

Cox, born in 1775, was a prosperous merchant and real estate owner who served as Mayor of the town for twenty-two years from 1823 to 1845. Well known as a dandy, he served as a Colonel during the War of 1812 and was thrice married; first to Matilda Smith, sister of the first president of the Farmers and Mechanics Bank. They had three children and this corner house is thought to have been the Cox residence during this period. His second wife was the daughter of John Threlkeld of Burleith, Mayor of Georgetown in 1793, and friend of Jefferson. Colonel and Mrs. Cox built a new house, "The Cedars," on part of the Threlkeld estate and were living here when Cox, as Mayor, entertained Lafayette in 1824.

As the arrival of one of the seven children born of this marriage was imminent, Colonel Cox had number 3337, next door to his former home and vacant at the time, completely furnished for the occasion. Even the edges of the floors were decorated by floral garlands drawn in colored chalk. His eldest daughter acted as hostess and a great supper was served which is supposed to have included 600 reed birds.

Number 3339 was at one time the home of Commodore Morris, a hero of the War of 1812, when he served as executive officer of the "Constitution" under Captain Isaac Hull. It was purchased in 1842 by James Keith for his daughter Mrs. Forrest. The old house, almost entirely unaltered, remained in the same family for over 100 years, until its recent purchase and fine restoration by John deBlois Wack.

Among the distinguished residents of the other five houses which make up the row have been William A. Gordon, once Chief of the Quartermaster Corps; Judge Robert Ould; Mayor Henry Addison; William Hunter, Assistant Secretary of State; William Laird, Jr., and many others.

*Photograph: Harris & Ewing*

One of the finest of its period

Tree shadows form a fascinating pattern on warm brick walls

*Photograph: Harris & Ewing*

Dormer. The grace and delicacy of its colonettes are in perfect harmony with the entrance door on the preceding page.

# THE McKENNEY HOUSE
## C. 1800
### 3123 Dumbarton Avenue

Unoccupied in recent years, this notable Federal house was built by Henry Foxall for his only daughter, Mary Ann, on her marriage to Samuel McKenney in 1800. It remained in the McKenney family until the death of Mary Ann Foxall McKenney's granddaughter, Mrs. McCartney,—then a grandmother—a few years ago. Enclosed by a low stone wall and white picket fence, it has fine dormers and a pillared porch with arched ceiling and gabled pediment. The interior trim is very fine.

One of the interesting inhabitants of the house in days gone by, was a spinster from Philadelphia who came for dinner, and being prevailed upon by the children to prolong her stay, remained for forty years until her death. She was somewhat eccentric and insisted that the candles be extinguished by ten o'clock—a peculiarity which her hosts allowed her. After her death, those who slept in the old lady's room found—strangely enough—that their candles went out precisely at ten o'clock; even when no drafts were present.

The old house, surrounded by its garden, is one of the few in Georgetown practically in its original condition. The recent years of desertion and neglect have not been kind to it, but it needs only a new owner with interest and sufficient funds to restore it to happier days again.

Even the luxuriant growth of **ivy cannot** completely mask the beauty of this house

## THE BERRY HOUSE
### 3100 Dumbarton Avenue, N. W.

This house, erected in 1810, was the home of Philip Taylor Berry in 1820. It survived a bad fire about 1900 and now, with the fine rear gallery cut off, and an addition to the west, is divided into apartments. Unfortunately the structure is now much higher above sidewalk level than it was originally, as a result of the cutting down of the street at this point. However, the garden is charming and the front doorway, with sidelights complementing the door panels, is very fine.

The original mantel with the design above it arranged by David Leavitt, well-known mural painter, to nullify the effect of the modern wall lights. The furniture displays similar classic feeling.

# THE TENNEY HOUSE
## C. 1805
## 3010 O Street, N. W.

Although part of it is much earlier, the portion of this charming frame house facing the street is thought to have been built in the first years of the Nineteenth Century by a Mr. Tenney who came to Georgetown from Newburyport, Massachusetts, about 1800. The white clapboards and the two end chimneys, in place of the great center type characteristic of its builder's native countryside, are an interesting adaptation of New England architecture to the warmer Maryland climate.

The house with its garden which originally extended to the corner was later the home of the builder's daughters, the three Misses Tenney and their sister Mrs. Brown, who conducted a school for small children. It was purchased in recent years by Major General Louis Mc-Carty Little, USMC. Mrs. Little, the internationally known decorator, Elsie Cobb Wilson, has restored it as a superb background for her fine collection of antique furniture and objects d'art.

Residence of Major General and Mrs. Louis McCarty Little

*Photograph: Harris & Ewing*

This charming doorway has been restored to its old form

*Photograph : Harris & Ewing*

From the garden—the house has grown through several additions

Another conversion from two rooms—hence two fireplaces

Photograph: Harris & Ewing

The other end of the Living Room. An unusually fine grouping of furniture of the period

*Photograph: Harris & Ewing*

These photographs show three walls of a beautiful small, partially panelled room, a restoration of an earlier period.

Photograph: Harris & Ewing

A portrait of General Little. The chinoiserie is some of the finest in the world

*Madame Bodisco*
Library of Congress photograph.

# THE BODISCO HOUSE
## C. 1820
## 3322 O Street, N. W.

The old Russian Legation is perhaps better known for its romantic history than for its severe and distinguished beauty. Here, at a fabulous Christmas party which he gave for his nephews, Waldemer and Boris, then students at Georgetown College, Baron Alexander de Bodisco, Imperial Russian Minister to the United States for the seventeen years before his death in 1854, met his future wife, the beautiful Harriet Brooke Williams. He immediately became infatuated with the blonde loveliness of the school girl of sixteen, and his sixty-two years seem in no way to have dampened the ardor and impetuosity of his courtship.

In spite of the opposition of the Williams family they were married in June 1849 at the home of the bride's mother. The bride was given away by Henry Clay and the groomsmen included Senator (later President) James Buchanan; Henry Fox, the British Minister; Mr. Martineau, the Netherlands Minister; Baron Saruyse, the Austrian Minister; Mr. Van Buren, son of the President; Mr. Forsythe, son of the Secretary of State; and Mr. Paulding, son of the Secretary of the Navy. A brilliant reception followed at the embassy where the bride in white and the groom in splendid court dress received a throng of distinguished guests including President Van Buren and Daniel Webster. However brief, the marriage was a very happy one. The great wealth of the Baron allowed him to shower his beautiful young wife with gorgeous jewels and gowns, and the house became famous for the gayety and magnificence of its entertaining.

The house is noteworthy for the severity of its lines, complemented by the great door, the fine pedimented portico, and the extremely graceful double stairway at the entrance. Extending to the side and rear is its spacious garden which, on the occasion of the Baron's lavish wedding reception, was specially decorated with lemon trees hanging full of golden fruit. It is thought that before its long period as a Legation, the house was occupied for a short time by the mother of General Robert E. Lee during his years at West Point. Later it was the home of Abraham Herr, and finally was used as an apartment until its purchase and sympathetic restoration by Francis C. de Wolf, the present owner.

*Photograph: Harris & Ewing*

A great eight-panelled door, delicate detail of portico, and recessed panels figure prominently in the superb design of this tall mansion; but its dignity is relieved by the wide sweep of its stairs—truly "opening arms."

# THE HARMON HOUSE
## C. 1810
### 3025 P Street, N. W.

The quaint little house which is now the home of Mr. and Mrs. Frank P. Harmon, was probably built about 1810. It is noteworthy for the fine stark simplicity of its exterior and for its sympathetically scaled interior trim.

Its later history is lacking, but the property was sold to Thomas and John Wirt in 1805. Between that date and 1816 deeds attest to its ownership at various times by Benjamin and John Pickrell, James and Henry Lunkins, R. Gaines, William Calder and Elisha Lanham.

It is likely that Mr. Calder built the house which was successively bought for investment purposes by Washington Bowie, the shipowner, in 1819 and by Francis Dodge in 1821. The latter had come to Georgetown from Salem as a youth in 1798. In the fifty-three years of his life in the town he became one of the greatest merchants and established one of its largest and most honored families in the huge old house which for many years dominated the block on which this little house still stands.

*Photograph: Harris & Ewing*

This close-up shows the house as a simple, straightforward expression of its purpose

*Photograph: Harris & Ewing*

Exquisite simplicity. Note the unusual square doorway and complementing details of the handrail.

*Photograph: Harris & Ewing*

Furniture in proper scale and the lovely soft colors make a perfect complement to this fine small house.

# THE LINTHICUM HOUSE
### 1826
## 3019 P Street, N. W.

The brick house standing at 3019 P Street was built in 1826 by one of Georgetown's three great philanthropists, Edward M. Linthicum, who lived here until 1846, when he purchased the large house built on Georgetown Heights by William H. Dorsey in 1801, now known as Dumbarton Oaks, but called "Monterey" by Linthicum in commemoration of the great battle of the Mexican War.

While Mr. Linthicum's later mansion became one of the famous estates of the District, this, his earlier home, is possibly a more perfect example of the taste and love of beauty for which this prosperous merchant and civic leader was well known. It is a superb example of the late Federal town house with a particularly fine doorway having both fan and side lights and an exquisite iron railing at the entrance steps. Directly on the street as are its neighbors, behind the house one finds a lovely garden which forms, with the others in the block, a great hollow square of lovely lawns, flowers and trees.

Mr. Linthicum, a merchant, member of the Town Council and trustee of the Methodist Church, left a legacy of $50,000 for the founding of a free school in Georgetown; being convinced, as he wrote, that knowledge and piety constitute the only assurance of happiness and healthful progress for the human race.

The fine house built by this good citizen became the home of Thomas Corcoran, Junior, an older brother of the financier and philanthropist W. W. Corcoran, who sold it to John R. Cochrane in 1856. The latter's sister, Mrs. James A. Magruder, and members of her family, lived here until its purchase by Victor Sutro who has restored it with unusual understanding.

The intriguing combination of white stone ornament and red brick wall is an interesting solution of the smaller house problem.

*Photograph: Harris & Ewing*

The filigree of shadows across this doorway is almost a match for the iron tracery of the handrail.

The Dining Room.  Peacock walls plus fine pine panelling of an earlier period

*Photograph: Harris & Ewing*

## THE MILLER HOUSE
### 1524 28th Street, N. W.

This small frame house was built about 1830 and was at one time the residence of Benjamin Miller of New York, designer and builder of the old Aqueduct Bridge across the Potomac. It is illustrated here as an interesting example of the general Georgetown type employing wood rather than the usual brick. It is distinctly reminiscent of houses of the era built in upper New York State and New England, yet it has the four end chimneys used in Georgetown and the surrounding locality. Its interior trim is noteworthy and its white clapboard walls and doric pillared porch are an interesting deviation from the typical Georgetown house of Federal type. It is today the home of Mr. and Mrs. R. F. Whitehead.

*Photograph: Harris & Ewing*

The charm of wood, well designed and well executed

# SEVIER PLACE
### 1800
## 3124 Q Street, N. W.

The south front of the dignified old mansion, built in 1800 by Washington Bowie, may be seen through a maze of boxwood and great trees from the old iron gates of the carriage entrance a block to the south. While the other facade, now high above Q Street is the finer in detail, this secluded garden seems to preserve the very atmosphere of the early Nineteenth Century. The house itself is characterized by very tall ceilings with fine plaster friezes, by finely carved mantels, and great mahogany doors. It has been extended and remodelled during the past fifty years, although the central mass retains the same appearance as when the estate covered the entire block on which it stands. Its builder, who was one of Georgetown's great shipowners, enjoyed the distinction of being a godson of General Washington, whose name is so closely linked with Tudor Place across Q Street. He was a member of the same family as Colonels James and Resin P. Bowie, respectively hero of the Alamo and inventor of the Bowie knife. In 1805 Mr. Bowie sold the property to William Nicholls of Maryland. His two daughters married W. F. Hanewinkel of Richmond and Colonel Hollingsworth, later Curator of Mount Vernon, whose names have since always been closely associated with it.

The old house was sold at auction in 1890 to Mr. and Mrs. John Sevier who happened to be visiting Georgetown at the time. He was the descendant and namesake of John Sevier, hero of Kings Mountain and first Governor of Tennessee. While they had spent a large part of their time abroad, they made this their permanent home, adding one wing to the house and extending the other. It has remained in the same hands ever since, and Mrs. Sevier plans for it to become a museum, similar to Dumbarton House, after her death.

There are wings of much later date but only the original house is shown here

# TUDOR PLACE
## C. 1815
## 1644 31st Street, N. W.

Tudor Place, aloof on its shaded lawns, is an unusual example of the Federal house of semi-rural type—unique in its distinguished history, its unbroken chain of family ownership, and its authenticity as one of the few Georgetown examples of the work of the distinguished architect-doctor, William Thornton. An exquisite example of the mansion type with extended wings, it is built of stuccoed brick of buff tone, accented by the white portico and trim, and is practically unchanged from its early appearance.

The property was originally purchased in 1794 from Thomas Beall by Francis Loundes who built the two story wings before he sold it in 1805 to Thomas Peter, Mayor of Georgetown from 1789 to 1798. Here, shortly after their marriage, the latter brought his bride, Martha Parke Custis, one of the three beautiful granddaughters of Martha Washington.

It is thought that the Peter's first used the west wing as their home and the east wing as a stable. In any case, Mrs. Peter decided to use the inheritance left her by the first President to build a mansion here, and the house was completed about 1816 according to Thornton's design. Here Lafayette was entertained when he visited Georgetown in 1824 and the house for many years became the background for a brilliant social scene stemming from the family's associations. Today it contains a notable collection of Washington family relics.

The south facade of the house is characterized by a masterful treatment of both mass and detail and is remarkable for the great main windows surmounted by arches, as well as for Thornton's two story "temple" or domed circular portico, half of which is a niche recessed into the center hall. The northern front, in contrast, is severely treated, and overlooks a circular "turn-around" and a great garden with fine old box. The north, or carriage entrance, opens into an unusual transverse hall backing three large rooms. Those at the sides contain handsome crystal chandeliers, delicate marble mantels, plaster friezes, and unusual doors of highly polished curly maple with great brass locks. The dining room, conservatory and kitchen are in the wings.

Mr. and Mrs. Peter, who built the mansion, had eight children. To Britannia the youngest child, and widow of Commodore Beverley Kennon, USN, who was killed in the tragic explosion aboard the U.S.S. Princeton in 1844, Mrs. Thomas Peter bequeathed Tudor Place. Mrs. Kennon, left a widow before she was thirty, lived to be ninety-six and died at Tudor Place in 1911. Her only child, Martha Custis Kennon, married her cousin, Dr. Armistead Peter, and thus the Peter name returned to this house which has never been out of the family. Today, it is the residence of their son, Armistead Peter, Jr.

*Photograph: Harris & Ewing*

The distinguished South front

*Photograph : Harris & Ewing*

The extreme simplicity of the North facade. Interesting contrast of formal box planting in the background and old-fashioned flower garden in the foreground.

*Photograph: Francis Benjamin Johnston*

Exquisite precision in a doorway

The Temple

This marble mantel and plaster frieze reflect Thornton's classic mood

93

# EVERMAY

## 1792

## 1623 28th Street, N. W.

One of the most beautiful sites in Georgetown is occupied by Evermay, built in 1792 by Samuel Davidson and now the residence of Mr. and Mrs. F. Lammot Belin.

Davidson, a bachelor, well known for his peculiarities, was a successful speculator in real estate, one of the proprietors of the District of Columbia, and with David Burns, owner of the land now occupied by the White House and Lafayette Park. He bequeathed his estate to his nephew Lewis Grant providing that he assumed the name of Davidson. The latter's daughter, Eliza Grant Davidson, who inherited the house, married Charles Dodge in a quadruple wedding June 12, 1847, and Evermay became another Dodge residence. On this occasion four of the Dodges were married at four o'clock in the morning in order that the bridal couples could take the five o'clock stage for Baltimore.

In the later Nineteenth Century the house was owned by the McPherson family and for many years was leased to William B. Orme. The present owners are responsible for its brilliant restoration and improvement. A coat of yellow stucco was removed from the house which was enlarged; the grounds were complemented with a brick wall and gatehouse, and a magnificent formal garden was created which is, in itself, a noteworthy collection of box, magnolia and azalea.

Its eccentric builder's desire to preserve the serenity of Evermay lives in his noteworthy advertisement of June 2, 1810, which forewarned "at their peril, all persons, of whatever age, color, or standing in society, from trespassing on the premises, in any manner, by day or by night; particularly all thieving knaves and idle vagabonds; all rambling parties; all assignation parties; all amorous bucks with their dorfies, and all sporting bucks with their dogs and guns"—and proclaimed, "For the information of those persons who may have real business on the premises, there is a good and convenient gate. But Mark! I do not admit mere curiosity as an errand of business. Therefore, I beg and pray of all my neighbors to avoid Evermay as they would a den of devils, or rattlesnakes, and thereby save themselves and me much vexation and trouble. Samuel Davidson."

*Photograph: Harris & Ewing*

There are wings of later date. However, this photograph shows only the original entrance facade.

The garden facade.   A formal brick house with superb detail

The garden doorway

*Photograph: Harris & Ewing*

A garden walk—Washington in the distance

Restoration planting at its best

Sky Tracery—Autumn

Spring Contrast

# DUMBARTON HOUSE

## C. 1805

## 2715 Q Street, N. W.

Dumbarton House, or Bellevue as it was called for a hundred-odd years before its purchase by the Colonial Dames in 1928, is possibly the earliest, and certainly one of the loveliest, of the "great houses" of Georgetown. It is a two-story mansion with extended wings, characteristic of the superior pattern of Georgian house popular in Eighteenth Century Maryland and Virginia for country living. It has the usual wide central hall with four large rooms opening into it. The mantels are fine and uniquely those rooms at the rear are oval at their outside ends. The wings are much simpler in treatment than the central mass with its longer windows and delicate fretwork beneath the cornice.

It was thought for a long time that the house was built about 1796 until investigations of old deeds and wills were made at the time of its purchase in 1928 by the Colonial Dames. Those in charge of the project deduced that a house as handsome as Bellevue would not have been built in its original location after the laying out of Georgetown. Addition of four more streets to the North and East of the town would have placed Bellevue at the convergence of two of them, and until the house was moved to its present site by the District Government in 1915 it stood directly in the middle of present-day Q Street.

It is now believed that part of the house was built by George Beall, the son of Ninian Beall, original proprietor of the "Rock of Dumbarton," about 1750. George Beall vigorously protested the founding of Georgetown, complaining that his property might be "totally demolished." He may well have had this house in mind, although no streets were laid out in close proximity until 1783 when his son Thomas, who had inherited this portion of his father's estate, made his first Addition to Georgetown. Moreover, the roof of Bellevue was in danger of falling in when it was leased by Samuel Whitall in 1820 and houses built as this was do not usually disintegrate to that extent in a mere forty or fifty years. In any case, the house in its present form bears close resemblance to handsome Tulip Hill built by the Galloways on West River near Annapolis about 1755 and to His Lordships Kindness near Rosaryville, built by the fourteenth Earl of Shrewsbury as a gift to his niece and ward, Ann Talbot, on her marriage to Henry Darnell.

The property changed hands several times in the feverish land speculation following the selection of the District of Columbia as site of the capital. In 1794 Thomas Beall sold Bellevue to Peter Casanave, who kept it for two months and resold it to Col. Forrest at twenty per cent profit. After a year the Colonel conveyed it to Isaac Pollack for five times its purchase price, but Pollack sold it the following year to Samuel Jackson at less than half its cost. Bellevue was then mortgaged, remortgaged, foreclosed, and finally sold in 1804 to Gabriel Duval, Comptroller of the Currency and later a Justice of the Supreme Court of the United States. In 1805 it passed to Joseph Nourse, Registrar of the Treasury, who remodeled it according to Latrobe's design and who lived there until 1813 when he sold it to Charles Carroll, who had purchased a paper mill on Rock Creek below the house with his brother Daniel of Duddington, and who thereafter styled himself "of Bellevue." According to legend, Mrs. Madison met the President here and agreed on the route of their retreat when the British burned the White House in 1814. Bellevue was leased to Samuel Whitall of Philadelphia in 1820 and was sold to his son by Carroll's executors in 1841. It subsequently was owned by the Rittenhouse family and the Hinkleys until its purchase by John L. Newbold in 1912. Shortly afterward it was moved to its present location and finally purchased and restored by the present owners.

Now handsomely furnished as of the period of 1790 to 1810, and complemented by beautiful gardens, this representative Georgian house has been open to the public until its recent temporary assignment to the Red Cross for war work.

The Central South facade as restored by the National Society of Colonial Dames

The semi-circular bays are emphasized in this view from the garden

*Photograph: Francis Benjamin Johnston. Courtesy Great Georgian Houses of America*

Furniture, mantel and bric-a-brac in perfect scale and harmony

*Photograph taken in 1943 showing 150 years accumulation of paint and architectural changes.*

# THE HYDE HOUSE
## C. 1798
### 1319 30th Street, N. W.

This house was built about 1798 by Charles Beatty who had purchased the lot on which it stands from Thomas Beall the year before. Colonel Beatty owned the ferry which plied the Potomac between the foot of Frederick (34th) Street and the Virginia shore, and in 1806 sold the house to Nicholas Hedges. It passed to James Belt in 1822 and to Joshua Stuart in 1832. The latter is thought to have added the present full third story, as well as a wing to the rear.

The house was later purchased by Thomas Hyde, an early merchant of the town, and was later the residence of his son, Anthony, for many years secretary to the distinguished philanthropist W. W. Corcoran. Recently when Deering Davis restored the house for Morehead Patterson he found a quaint old sign bearing the following bit of doggerel and dating back to the elder Hyde:

> *"Hyde's my name, and Hides I buy*
> *3¢ for wet and 5¢ for dry."*

The small photograph above shows the house as it was in 1943 before restoration began. On page 107 one sees the structure as it now appears and almost as it was in 1797. However the roof was originally of steeper pitch and extended to just above the second story windows. The third floor plan was as it is today but the windows were dormers. About 1830 the roof line was changed and the facade extended to include them. More than 20 coats of paint were removed by steam and chemicals to recover the original fine salmon colored brick. Now the house looks almost too new and passersby remark on the difficulties that must have been encountered in painting all the joint lines white, little realizing that the lime mortar is almost 150 years old.

*Photograph: Harris & Ewing*

Photograph taken in 1944 illustrates perfectly a restoration to its original state of 1798

The house has original panelled doors of perfect scale with old locks of almost jewel-like refinement. For years they were covered and caked with numerous coats of paint.

An unusual reeded stair panel of waxed red pine running to the third floor. The plain painted panels underneath are typical of the Post-Revolutionary Period in contrast to the raised and bev-**eled** type of earlier date. Note original wide pine flooring.

# GEORGE WASHINGTON'S HOUSES ON CAPITOL HILL

In the Eighteenth Century an interest in architecture and a taste for decoration seem to have been almost universal characteristics of the gentry. Jefferson's abilities in these directions are well known. Old letters, architectural libraries, estates and houses of the period testify to similar interests on the part of his contemporaries. While Washington inferred in several letters to Dr. Thornton that he was ignorant of architectural principles and claimed that he had "no other guide but his eye," in the same letters he discusses features of two houses which he wished to have built in the new national capital with deep perception and judgment that belie his claims. Other writings as well as the details of the classic state dining room and west parlor which he added to his inheritance, Mount Vernon, are adequate indications of his taste and interest.

The outstanding architects of the day were employed by the leaders of the young Republic to build both public and domestic buildings. In this connection the fact that President Washington engaged Dr. William Thornton to design two private houses for him on Capitol Hill becomes of particular interest. The same architects, of course, designed the outstanding buildings in both Georgetown and Washington itself, but documentary evidence of the work is almost entirely confined to public structures or large houses of mansion or manor type, such as Octagon House and Tudor Place. With few exceptions, the smaller type of town dwelling found in Georgetown, the subject of most of the preceding illustrations, cannot be connected authentically with any prominent architect, even though legend attributes many of them to Dr. Thornton.

These houses were so simple in mass and such a direct adaptation of a well established English prototype that any competent carpenter-contractor could and did build them. However, the design of both exterior and interior trim and detail was copied exactly and directly from the best examples of the known works of Thornton, Hoban and Latrobe.

Therefore, newly discovered details of the building and design of two such town houses actually planned for the first President by William Thornton, the most influential of these architectural leaders, who first planned the new Capitol and whose work there General Washington actively supported, becomes particularly significant.

Several writers have claimed that Dr. Thornton built a double house on Capitol Hill for the President in 1792 or 1793 where he lived for part of three years, stopping on his return from Philadelphia at the close of Congressional sessions to examine the progress of the erection of the Capitol building. These seem to be perfectly reasonable statements, but further research has uncovered several letters written in December 1798 and August and September 1799 giving definite details of the two houses for which Thornton was actually architect and supervisor of construction during the last two years of the President's life. Another letter of Washington's to Alexander White speaks of these houses, indicating that they were being built as an investment as well as for the convenience of Members of Congress, for whom adequate lodging was so difficult to obtain, and stating that at a later date the President would perhaps build a town house for his personal use. Although he had purchased some lots in that section of Washington in 1792 and 1793 the combination of letters mentioned above dispels any thesis that Washington had a residence in the District and that his letters to Thornton referred to two additional houses he wished to build. Washington wrote as follows:

To William Thornton.

(See complete original letter page 114)

Dear Sir,

Mount Vernon
Dec. 20th, 1798

I saw a building in Philadelphia of about the same dimensions in front and elevation that are to be given to my two houses,—which pleased me.—It consisted also of two houses, united Doors in the center, a Pediment in the Roof and dormer windows on each side of it in front, skylight in the rear.—

If this is not incongruous with rules of Architecture, I should be glad to have my two houses executed in this style.

* * * * * *

To William Thornton

Dear Sir,

Mount Vernon,
30th Dec. 1798

Your favor of the 25th. instant, enclosing Messrs. Blagden & Leuthals estimate of the cost of adding a Pediment, and Parapet to the roof of my buildings in the Federal City, has been duly received, but the plan, to which it refers, did not accompany it.—

This plan, on other accounts, I ought to be possessed of, and Mr. Blagden is under promise to take a copy thereof for his own use, to work by, and to send me the original draught.—I pray you to remind him of this promise.—

Presuming that it is not necessary for Mr. Blagden's convenience that I should, at this moment, decide upon the above estimate; nor whether I shall adopt the measure at all; I shall, if no disadvantage will attend the delay, suspend my determination until I can visit the City, & receive some further explanations respecting the consequent alterations which will be occasioned by this Pediment—not at present well understood by me; owing to my entire ignorance of the technical terms in which they are expressed.—At which time also, I will make arrangements for giving him further pecuniary aid.

Rules of Architecture are calculated, I presume, to give symmetry, and just proportion to all the Orders, & parts of buildings, in order to please the eye.—Small departures from strict rules are discoverable only by skilful architects, or by the eye of criticism; while ninety-nine in a hundred—deficient of their knowledge—might be pleased with things not quite orthodox.—This, more than probable, would be the case relative to a Pediment in the Roof over the doors of my houses in the City.—

That a Parapet in addition (for the reasons you have assigned) would have a pleasing & useful effect, cannot be doubted.—When the roof of a building is to be seen—and when it is designed for Chambers it must be seen—something to relieve the view of a plain and dead Surface, is indispensable:—for this reason it was, I thought, and still do think that Dormars are to be preferred to Sky lights in the front;—on the other hand, if the roof is so flat as not to be seen at all, or so low as, in a manner to be hid by a Parapet, I should give a decided preference to Sky lights.—

These ideas, as you will readily perceive, proceed from a person who avows his ignorance of Architectural principles,—and who has no other guide but his eye, to direct his choice:—I never, for a moment, contemplated two Pediments, one over the door of each house, my great object was to give them the appearance of one.—But as I have observed in the former part of this letter, I will suspend coming to any decision until the consequences of the proposed alterations are better understood by me.—

The freedom with which you have expressed your sentiments on this occasion, is highly pleasing to me.—Sorry indeed should I have been on this, as I shall be on any future occurrence, when your opinion may be asked, if they are not rendered with the utmost frankness and candour.—

The compliments of the season are presented to Mrs. Thornton, yourself & Co. by all parts of this family,—and with great esteem and regard I remain, &c.

* * * * * *

To John Francis.

Mount Vernon,
Aug. 25, 1799.

Cost of two Lots in the Federal City, extending from North Capitol Street to New Jersey Avenue in Square 634, together with the expense of the Buildings now erecting thereon, according to

111

Contract; and an estimate of work not included in the said Contract, occasioned by alterations agreed on since.

viz

Dollars

For lot No. 16, bought from the Commissioners ................................. 535.71
" " " 7, " " Mr. Daniel Carroll** ................................ 428.40

On the price of these lots considerable abatement was made, on condition of my building *two* brick houses *three* stories high each.

To Mr. Blagden, Undertaker of the Buildings, according to written Contract. Estimate of Glazing, Painting and Ironmougry* } 11,250.00

Conceiving these charges were high, in the estimate, *I took them, upon myself. But whether I shall lose by so doing, remains to be decided. Mr. Blagden assured me he could not obtain them on better terms than was specified ** of Duddington.

Glazing and Painting, agreeably to this estimate handed in by Mr. Blagden, but not agreed to, nor included in Contract ................................................ 840.00
Ironmongry Ditto—Do—Do ......................................................... 397.20

A well of fine water at the back doors of both houses; 30 odd feet deep, walled, and a pump therein; the cost of which has not been exhibited, as it was procured to be done by Mr. Blagden, and paid for by him, out of the monies advanced him for general purposes. ........................................................................ .........

A Pediment and Parapet, in addition to the original cost of the Buildings. No specific sum agreed on for erecting them ............................................... .........

Carried over    $13,451.31

Cost of two lots brought over ...................................................... 13,451.31
...For the original design of.....to add to the appearance of the House: also undefined in the cost ......................................................................... .........
Papering all the Rooms, except Cellars and garrets,....being, by Contract to have to... of Plaster than is merely sufficient for that purpose. ................................ .........

*The press copy was poorly made. Words indicated by leaders are illegible.

Writings of Washington Col. 37, Nov. 1798-Dec. 1799.

*   *   *   *   *   *

To Wm. Thornton

Mt. Vernon<br>Oct. 1, 1799

Painters finding all materials, will do the windows, and cornice, and doors, in short all the exterior of the Buildings, the roof excepted (which must remain for future decision) upon the Terms, etc.

*   *   *   *   *   *

To John Avery

Mt. Vernon,<br>Sept. 25, 1799.

(In part)

Although my house, or houses (for they may be one or two as occasion requires) are, I believe upon a larger scale than any in the vicinity of the Capitol, yet they fall far short of your wishes. The largest room, and that occasionally made so, is not more than 40 (sic) feet in length. The houses are three flush stories of Brick, besides Garret rooms; and in the judgment of those better acquainted in these matters than I am capable of accommodating between twenty and thirty boarders. The buildings are not costly, but elegantly plain and the whole cost, at pretty near guess, may be between 15 and 16 thousand dollars.

*   *   *   *   *   *

Further search has brought to light the photograph of this famous double house with many changes, shown on page 117. It had obviously been converted into a five story hotel with a Mansard roof. When great granite blocks were being hauled for the construction of the Senate wing of the Capitol, the road was much cut down to ease the grade and facilitate the task. This bank was then cut into, and two stories were added underneath the house while the roof was changed to the Mansard type. A better picture was finally discovered which appears on page 116, and shows a third house nearest the camera. This house can be seen at the extreme left with its original entrance undoubtedly similar to the others. Interestingly enough Thornton used similar Ionic columns in the entrance of Octagon House.

The illustration on page 115 shows an interpretation of the front elevation of the two houses as ordered by George Washington who died a few months before their completion in 1799. The day following the Battle of Bladensburg in 1814 they were burned, but the walls remained, and in 1818 these houses were rebuilt. Only four years had passed so that the memory of their appearance must have been very clear and as Dr. Thornton was still active they were undoubtedly restored to their original exterior condition except for the omission of pediment and parapet, the changing of the window lintels and the addition of a string course. The pediment and parapet were not restored in all probability, both to save expense and because the houses were to be used for boarders and the dormers gave additional space and light to the garret rooms. In the rendered drawing the design of the window lintels has been changed from those in the photographs, since the key type of lintel rather than the end block form, was used in all buildings authentically attributed to Thornton. The plaques were also typical of his work.

These buildings were razed in 1913 and we are indebted to the historical interest of two Massachusetts officers for the picture of the houses as they appeared at the time of the Civil War. It was at their request that Brady, the great photographer, took the plate in 1863, and preserved a pictorial record of the only two authentically documented Thornton town houses of the smaller type so popular in Georgetown.

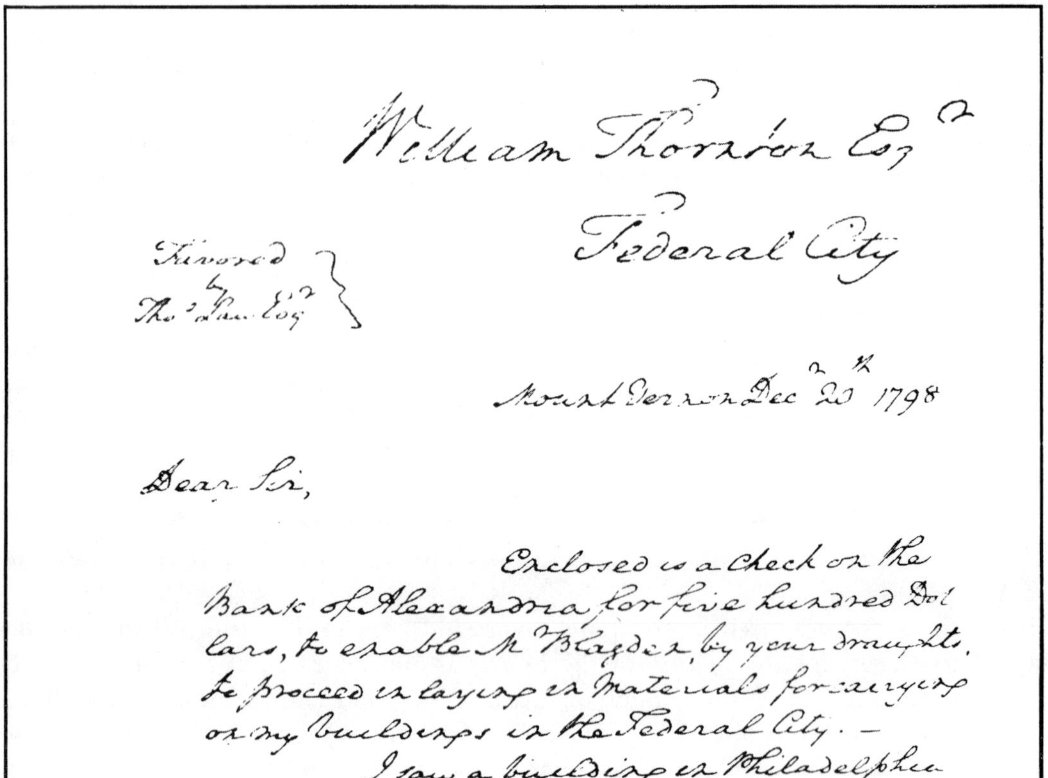

William Thornton Esq.
Federal City

Favored
by
Tho.s Law Esq.

Mount Vernon Dec.r 20.th 1798

Dear Sir,

Enclosed is a check on the
Bank of Alexandria for five hundred Dol
lars, to enable M.r Blagden, by your draughts,
to proceed in laying in materials for carrying
on my buildings in the Federal City. —
I saw a building in Philadelphia
of about the same front & elevation, that are
to be given to my two houses, which pleased
me. — It consisted also of two houses united,
— Doors in the centre — a pediment in the roof,
and dormar window on each side of it in
front — Skylights in the rear.
If this is not incongruous with rules
of architecture, I should be glad to have my
two houses executed in this style — Let me
request the favor of you to know from M.r
Blagden what the additional cost will be
I am — Dear Sir
Your most Obed.t & hble Serv.t
G. Washington

W.m Thornton Esq.

By permission of the Columbia Historical Society. Library of Congress Photograph

Photograph of letter.   The signature of this letter is unassailable documentary evidence verifying the facts of this chapter.

Illustrations on pages 116-117, plus the letters on pages 111-112 clearly demonstrate that this drawing shows the original appearance of the distinguished double house ordered by George Washington.

 **Cut** this house in half, remove Pediment, substitute Dormers for Parapet and the prototype of a typical Georgetown house clearly emerges.

This photograph was taken in 1861 and shows George Washington's double house as it was rebuilt in 1818, after burning in 1814. There is a third house at the end nearest the camera.

The street much cut down to haul the granite blocks, so plainly visible, is shown on preceding page. The face of the hill was cut away and two stories added underneath to create this five story hotel with added Mansard roof, more dormers, fire escapes, etc.

# THE PRE-REVOLUTIONARY DWELLINGS

Georgetown's days of glory were encompassed within the limits of the last quarter of the Eighteenth and the first quarter of the Nineteenth Centuries. It was during this period that the characteristic Federal Houses, for which she is noted, developed; yet any comprehensive account of this town's great architectural idiom, would be incomplete if it did not cover briefly the local antecedents from which its features were derived.

The ordinary conception of Georgetown houses as "Colonial" is, as already indicated, quite erroneous, as few pre-revolutionary structures remain standing. There were perhaps fifty good brick houses in the town in 1775. Of these and their frame counterparts, with the exception of minor portions of later structures, only six authentic examples remain—all, in bad residential areas. Before these few are lost entirely, it is regrettable that several are not moved to good locations and intelligently restored. Already two have been so completely gutted that nothing but the original walls remain. While there are a number of other dwellings—or more correctly parts thereof,—bearing the legend of a building date before 1775, they have been so altered in every exterior and interior feature, that one can only say that their present appearance is that of a considerably later period. Certainly this excludes them from the company of houses which clearly demonstrate the distinct style of the local Colonial or earlier Georgian period.

To the discerning eye there are distinct differences in the exterior appearance of houses built before and after the Revolution. The characteristic local idiom of the post-revolutionary period has already been discussed. In structures of the preceding era bricks are less regular and more obviously of hand moulded origin. The roof angle is generally more pronounced, window openings may have flat arches, and there is usually a water table beneath the principal story capped by an extended course of hand shaped bricks. Dormer details, window size and trim and entrance door details are quite different. Siding in frame structures, is generally of great width. In fact, it is the wood trim both within and without which shows such marked variance that a modicum of serious training is necessary to enable one to distinguish between products of the two epochs with reasonable ease.

The famous stone house on M Street shown on page 120 has been the subject of countless legends and disputes over its identity as Washington's Engineering headquarters and as the renowned Suter's Tavern. In any case, we do know that it was built about 1765 by Christopher Lehman, that it was frequently rented, and that it once served as an ordinary of which Cassandra Chew was at one time proprietess. Its interior paneling and trim is good but rather obviously transplanted to this house from an earlier location. It is of ell shape and the stone terminates at the eave line—the gable ends being of brick. A similar variation in the bonds used may be seen in the treatment of some of the very early Virginia country houses of simple brick type. The large twenty-light window on the ground floor is somewhat reminiscent of those in Alexandria's Ramsey House built in 1755. It is interesting that Washington's small Alexandria town house—recently demolished, shocking as the fact is —was strikingly similar to the Lehman house.

One of the other dwellings is of frame construction. The tiny cottage on 28th Street, now so gaily painted dark blue and yellow, was built prior to 1775 and has remained almost unchanged in a wonderful state of preservation—a tribute to the craftsmen who built it, and the honest timbers used. The extreme width of the hand hewn boards (shown on the ex-

3001 and 3003 M Street

3049 M Street                                    1222 28th Street

posed end) of the house on page 120 is impressive in an age when great forest timbers are no longer a characteristic of the country.

Of the remaining five, the two brick houses at the corner of 30th and M Streets, shown on page 119 are the finest examples of late pre-revolutionary buildings in the town. The interior trim still extant on the second floor is excellent, and the houses carry the characteristic water table mentioned above, oddly enough, between the first and second stories. Uniquely one of the window openings to be seen in the illustration is topped by a flat arch.

Exhaustive research indicates that these two houses were originally one, a very fine 2½ story mansion house of the Maryland type. The street level has been cut down so that the former basement is now the street level shops as shown in plate. The unusual placement of the water table mentioned above is thus accounted for.

The great significance of these houses lies in their early contribution to the American Architectual tradition. Such structures are becoming more scarce with each passing year. Surely more active measures should be taken to preserve the remaining earlier homes of our forefathers that are still spared.

# STRUCTURES NOW STANDING IN GEORGETOWN ERECTED BEFORE 1825

An accurate list of all structures still standing in the town, erected during the Georgian and early Federal period is extremely difficult to compile. It is expected that omissions in the following—particularly of smaller frame structures—will be found and that some readers will disagree with certain dates in connection with individual buildings.

The site, originally situated in part of Prince George's County, Maryland (organized from part of Charles County in 1695), became part of Montgomery County when it was created in 1776. The town, although organized in 1751, was not incorporated until 1789, and did not give up its charter of separate government, which it had kept even after inclusion in the District of Columbia, until 1871. Records are therefore scanty and scattered, and many have been lost.

Consequently dates with any documentary semblance of accuracy are unobtainable in a great many cases. Thus no dates are given where tradition or research have not afforded reasonable ones in conformity with the original architectural detail of the structure in question. Buildings no longer standing, unrecognizably altered, or containing a very slight portion of the original, as in the case of the Key Mansion, have not been included.

## M STREET AND WISCONSIN AVENUE
### (Formerly Bridge and High Streets)

These streets, which are primarily commercial today, contain a number of structures which are evidently of this approximate period. Except where otherwise noted they are of brick construction (usually only the fronts are of Flemish bond), of two or three stories and attic, the majority with two or four end chimneys. In every case they are today business or commercial buildings, frequently dilapidated, often almost unrecognizably altered. Most of them are characterized by one or two dormers of widely varying architectural worth and states of repair, and occasional remnants of good architectural detail. Regrettably, those with the most interesting historical associations have been completely razed.

M Street—Numbers 2803, 2919, 3001, 3003, 3005, 3009, 3026, 3041, 3049 (Christopher Lehman House, built by him in 1764 of field stone with brick gables. This small story and a half house of ell shape, with steep pitched roof and dormers is reminiscent of Williamsburg. Its ceilings are low and the rooms are small. Traditionally Washington's engineering headquarters when he planned the Federal city with L'Enfant, the authenticity of this legend has been disputed for many years.) 3053, 3064, 3066, 3068, 3112, 3116, 3204, 3209, 3211, 3232 (clapboard), 3249, 3264, 3350 (built in 1791 by Col. Uriah Forrest, then Mayor. In 1830 it became the home of William Marbury, and is now greatly changed).

Wisconsin Avenue—Numbers 1211, 1218, 1220, 1221, 1255 (John Lutz House—now a home for aged women); N. W. corner of Wisconsin and M Streets (interesting corner store built in 1817 for W. W. Corcoran & Co.);

1322 and 1324 (originally one clapboard house with heavy center chimney), 1503 (clapboard), 1507, 1515, 1517, 1522, 1524, 1525, 1529, 1611.

This area, where most of the business activity of the town took place before 1800, is today a region of warehouses, industrial buildings, and dilapidated early structures. Bordering the old Chesapeake and Ohio Canal as it does, it has a unique charm of its own, and there are encouraging signs in the recent renovation of some of its neglected houses, which are generally of much smaller scale than those on or above M Street. Because of its homogeneous character this section of the town has been treated here as if it were one street. Interesting structures of the period are to be found at the following addresses:

3037 K Street (formerly Wapping). A warehouse.

K Street—Second warehouse from the corner of Wisconsin Avenue.

K Street (old West Lane Keys) between Cecil Alley and Potomac Street. A three-story warehouse. The Eastern section has a water table characteristic of pre-Revolutionary houses and was probably erected ca 1760. The roof line has been changed.

K Street (formerly Water Street) between 33rd and 34th Streets. A large four story warehouse, ca 1790.

1068 and 1070 30th Street (formerly Washington Street). Two interesting one story brick cottages, each with two dormers.

1058 Jefferson Street, Potomac Masonic Lodge No. 5. This small building with dilapidated classic facade, stands next to the Canal and was built in 1810. The Lodge participated in the laying of the cornerstone of the Capitol, September 18, 1793.

1041 Jefferson Street—Simple two story brick house.

1063, 1067, 1071, 1074, 1076 Jefferson Street. Five small two story houses with dormered attics.

1006, 1008, 1010 Wisconsin Avenue (formerly Water Street). Group of three fine old warehouses. The center building is thought to have been built about 1770.

1066 Wisconsin Avenue (formerly Water Street). Vigilant Firehouse. Built ca 1825 on the edge of the Canal. Now a store.

1052 and 1060 Potomac Street. Small two story houses with dormered attics.

1041 33rd Street (formerly Duck Lane). Two story house of clapboard construction with great center chimney.

## PROSPECT STREET

3400—STODDERT HOUSE.

Benjamin Stoddert, first Secretary of the Navy, built this house in 1783. Regrettably altered by nondescript additions, only its southern facade shows the fine original center mass with its smaller wings. Some of the boxwood in the southern terrace is over 150 years old, and the view of the river is unequalled.

3425—WORTHINGTON HOUSE.

This notable brick house of ell shape with fine doorway and cornice was built by John Thomson Mason in 1798 and was sold to John Teakel in 1807. Bought by Dr. Charles Worthington in 1810 and named "Quality Hill," it was transferred to James Kearney in 1840. Unoccupied for many years it is now being restored.

3508—TEMPLEMAN HOUSE.

Built overlooking the river in 1788 by John Templeman and later the home of Lt. Comdr. Geo. Upham Morris, the house is beautifully restored. The front has fine Georgian detail and the octagonal watchtower at the rear is unique. The galleries above the terrace, with their leaf and grape design, are later additions.

## N STREET

### (Formerly Gay and First Streets)

2721, 2723, 2725—Two story houses of ell-shape with dormered attics. The first and last are much altered.

2806—(See detailed account, page 24).

2808—JOHN STODDERT HAW HOUSE. (See detailed account, page 30).

2811—A fine two story and attic house of frame construction with gambrel roof. ca 1795.

2812—DECATUR HOUSE. (See detailed account, page 36).

2823—ADMIRAL WEAVER HOUSE.

(Supposed to be pre-Revolutionary) with the exception of the south front built about 1835.

2900—Built ca 1810, this house of three stories with attic dormers was once the residence of Mrs. Williamson, daughter of Rev. Stephen Bloomer Balch. It has a fine doorway and is slightly altered by a Palladian window to the left of the doorway.

2908—FOXALL HOUSE. (See detailed account, page 44).

3014—LAIRD-DUNLOP HOUSE. 1799. (See detailed account, page 48).

3017—THOMAS BEALL HOUSE. 1794.

Built as an investment, and oddly enough typical of New England seacoast mansions of the Federal era, Major George Peter purchased it in 1811 and it was later owned by John Laird, Wm. Redin and John D. Smoot. It was the residence of Newton D. Baker when he was Secretary of War.

3033—GEORGE BEALL HOUSE.

The central portion, which is asserted to have been built by Colonel George Beall before the Revolution, presently shows no characteristics of such early date. It is composed of a twelve foot hall with two twenty foot square rooms opening on it from the east. The second story is the same and the dormered third floor was finished as two rooms. The east wing was added in 1871 and the west wing and veranda were added later. George Beall (died 1780) and his wife (died 1748) were once buried in a family plot formerly to the east of the house. Thomas Beall is thought to have inherited this house in 1780, and it was subsequently the home of Mrs. Robert Peter and John Cox.

3038—RIGGS-RILEY HOUSE. ca 1805. (See detailed account, page 50).

3241—Probably built about 1820 this ell-shaped dwelling is somewhat neglected and greatly altered by a mansard roof and other victorian additions.

3249—Built ca 1820, this house, although marred by victorian alterations, has a fine arched doorway with semicircular transom and one unusual side light.

3255 to 3263—COLONEL JAMES SMITH ROW. ca 1805.

Fine examples of the Federal type of row house with classic dormers and recessed panels relieving the facade, built by Colonel Smith about the same time as Cox's Row.

3265, 3267—These identical houses were built by John Marbury, and are of three stories with attic dormers. Considerably altered.

3302—BALCH HOUSE. ca 1820.

This house, with rear wing and gallery, was the last residence of Rev. Stephen Bloomer Balch, beloved and militant Presbyterian minister of early Georgetown.

3304—A duplicate of the Balch House. ca 1820.

3308, 3310, 3312, 3314, 3316, 3318, 3320—Two "rows" of three and four houses respectively, built about 1820 of three story and attic dormer type. Numbers 3314 and 3320 have been regrettably altered by victorian additions.

3309 and 3311—Two houses, ca 1810, much changed by victorian alterations.

3331 to 3339—Cox's Row. ca 1805. (See detailed account, page 58).

3402—Small two story frame house with great center chimney and plaster front.

3525—CONVENT OF MERCY.

Built 1787-1792 as Trinity Church, the first Catholic Church in the District of Columbia.

3700—OLD NORTH BUILDING, Georgetown University, erected ca 1790. From its steps George Washington made a brief address in 1796.


## DUMBARTON AVENUE

2613—A simple two story house.

2801—A simple house of brick and frame construction, ca 1810, now a store.

3040—Once the home of Jeremiah Williams and later of the Edes and Mackall families. Originally of two story and dormer type, now considerably enlarged and altered.

3100—BERRY HOUSE.

This house, erected in 1810, was the home of Philip Taylor Berry in 1820. It survived a bad fire about 1900 and with the fine rear gallery cut off, is now divided into apartments.

3123—McKENNEY HOUSE. (See detailed account, page 62).

3139—The rear portion was built about 1810, but it has been greatly enlarged by subsequent additions.

3143, 3145, 3147—Originally simple two story and attic dwellings.


## O STREET

### (Formerly Beall and Second Streets)

3010—WILLIAM H. TENNEY HOUSE. (See detailed account, page 66).

3017—COMMODORE CASSIN HOUSE. ca 1810.

This tall three story house has a fine doorway with side lights and arched overdoor, and a gallery to the east. It has a small door yard with fine old box and is altered only by victorian grills at the lower windows.

3112—A brick two story dwelling with attic dormers. ca 1810.

3114—A two story house with dormers. Probably built about 1810 and altered.

3122—A three story house—late Eighteenth Century.

3125—A three story house originally of two story and dormer type. ca 1805.

3126—Greatly altered, this house built in 1810 was the old Lancastrian School, later known as the Osborne house.

3130, 3132—Probably built about 1820, these houses of three stories have good attic dormers.

3131—A small two story house, ca 1805.

3213, 3216—Simple brick two story houses.

3240—SAINT JOHN'S EPISCOPAL CHURCH.

This church was completed in 1809 from plans by Dr. William Thornton, architect of the Capitol by subscribers headed by Thomas Jefferson. It is now considerably changed by a reduction in height of the octagonal steeple, stained glass, plastered walls and other neo-Gothic additions.

3245—GREGG HOUSE.

This small house, built before 1820, is of extremely simple style and has been well restored.

3322—BODISCO HOUSE. ca 1805. (See detailed account, page 74).

3328—A low two story brick house set back from the street. Probably built about 1820.


## P STREET

### *(Formerly West and Third Streets)*

2811—A three story and attic house with dormer, built about 1820 and slightly altered by an early victorian doorway and entrance stair.

2928—A three story house with good doorway. ca 1820.

3019—LINTHICUM HOUSE. 1826. (See detailed account, page 80).

3021—Built ca. 1800, this two story brick house with dormered attic was once the home of Horatio Berry. The doorway has been altered.

3023—A two story dwelling with attic dormers similar to 3021. ca. 1800.

3025—A two story brick house built about 1825. (See detailed account, page 76).

3022-3026—Two houses, three stories, part of a row of five, built ca. 1810, and at various times homes of the Magruder, Kenyon, Yarnell and Fowler families. These were rebuilt after a fire in 1860.

3028, 3030, 3034—Three houses, part of the same row, built ca. 1810, in original condition.

3033, 3035—A brick double house with greatly altered attic dormers, built about 1810.

3044—A simple two story brick house, probably built about 1820.

3101—Once the home of General Otho Holland Williams, built ca. 1800—now an apartment building and greatly changed.

3103—An interesting brick structure, one room deep; part of the Williams house. The doorway with side and fan lights opens onto a small walled garden at the side.

3108—MORSELL HOUSE. ca. 1815.

Built by Judge Morsell, this house of three stories with attic dormers, was successively the home of the Barnards, of the Marquis de Podestad, the Spanish Minister, and of General George C. Thomas.

3116—Three story brick house. ca. 1820.

3122—A two story brick house with attic dormers, built about 1810.

3142—TENNEY HOUSE. ca. 1810.

This handsome dwelling of two stories with dormered attic and wings, has been ably enlarged and restored. It incorporates the old house of the Rev. Mr. Stephenson and has a lovely garden to the rear.

3232—A small tenement of two stories.

3267—A simple house of ell shape—originally of two stories—much altered.

3270—A small house of three stories and ell shape, with excellent detail, probably built about 1810.

3323—Probably built about 1810, with a full third story and long ell added later. Now badly defaced by Victorian alterations.

3327—Built about 1820, this tall house of four stories and plaster front has a fine doorway with sidelights and fan.

3512—A two story brick house with dormered attic. ca. 1798.


## Q STREET
### *(Formerly Stoddard and Fifth Streets)*

2715—BELLEVUE, now DUMBARTON HOUSE. Built ca. 1750; enlarged 1805. (See detailed account, page 102).

3124—BOWIE HOUSE, now SEVIER PLACE. Built 1805, enlarged 1890. (See detailed account, page 86).


## R STREET
### *(Formerly Road and Eighth Streets)*

3101—DUMBARTON OAKS.

The main house was built in 1801 by William H. Dorsey, appointed first Judge of the Orphans Court by President Jefferson. It was sold in 1805 to Robert Beverley whose son James transferred it as "Acrolophos House" to James E. Calhoun in 1823. Lafayette was entertained here and it became the home of John C. Calhoun during his term as Vice President. It was bought by Brooke Mackall in 1826 and by Edward Linthicum, who named it "Monterey" in 1846. Its next owner, Col. Henry M. Blount, renamed it "The Oaks." The exterior is altered by a mansard roof and by two new wings, and the interior is similarly changed. Until recently the home of Robert Woods Bliss, former Minister to Argentina; since 1940 it has been the property of Harvard University. Given by the Blisses as a research center and enriched by their great collection of Byzantine Art, it stands among great trees surrounded by 16 acres of noteworthy gardens.

3406—MACKALL-WORTHINGTON HOUSE.

Built by Leonard Mackall in 1820 and later owned by the Worthingtons. It has a lovely garden, but has been altered by a mansard roof, bracketed cornice, etc.


## 28th STREET
### *(Formerly Montgomery Street)*

1222—A tiny clapboard cottage now much below street level. Its roof is of steep pitch with dormers. Probably built before the Revolution.

1301—This house, although well restored, is much altered. It is of two stories with dormered attic. ca. 1800.

Southeast Corner of Dumbarton Avenue. OLD AUGUR HOUSE, ca. 1795. Now regrettably altered.

1314-1318—Two simple types of three stories with dormered attics, built about 1810. The first has been restored.

1352 and Southwest Corner of O Street. Two simple three story houses of ell shape. **ca. 1820.** Much altered by Victorian additions. Originally they were of two story and dormer type.

1524—MILLER HOUSE. ca. 1830. (See detailed account, page 84).

1623—EVERMAY. 1792. (See detailed account, page 94).


## 29th STREET

### (Formerly Greene Street)

1308—A small brick dwelling, restored and much enlarged. Of two stories and attic it has dormers, brick corbel table, and a doorway with side lights and arched transom.

1332—A very small house of two stories.

1633—MACKALL SQUARE.

The main portion of this old house, (only one room in depth) set among fine old trees, was built ca. 1820 by Benjamin Mackall. The classic portico was built at the same time and is similar to Latrobe's at Dumbarton House. The wing to the rear terminates in a very old one story clapboard cottage with attic dormers, small six light windows, roof of steep pitch and great fireplace, is apparently of mid-Eighteenth Century construction.


## 30th STREET

### (Formerly Washington Street)

1204-1204½-1208-1210—The first two of these four houses (three of them of the three story and dormered attic type) were probably built about 1770, the others about 1800. Both number 1208 and 1210 have fifteen light windows and the former has been well restored. The other two houses have been somewhat altered. Number 1204½ has a unique wide 12 light dormer.

1241—A New England type with great center chimney, probably built about 1815. The first story is of brick, the second frame, and it is set with its gable to the street.

1300—A three story house of ell shape altered by a mansard roof.

1302—Once a duplicate of 1300, it is badly altered by a Victorian mansard and tower.

1305-1315—COLONIAL APARTMENTS.

Considerably altered, this building was once part of Miss Lydia English's Female Seminary, built ca. 1820. It was a union hospital during the Civil War.

1319—MATTHEW HYDE HOUSE. ca. 1798. (See detailed account, page 106).

1325-1327—Originally one low house of two stories with great center chimney and two dormers. Lintels have raised end blocks. Built about 1820.

1330—DE LA ROCHE HOUSE. Built ca. 1820 this frame house was the residence of Captain De la Roche, early architect and is much altered.

1344—This beautiful dwelling has been reconstructed from three old houses built about 1810. It is greatly altered but has handsome gardens.

1647—BEALL-WASHINGTON HOUSE.

This house, facing R Street and set in fine grounds, was built by Thomas Beall, ca. 1784. Successively the home of his sons-in-law Col. George Corbin Washington, great nephew of the President and of Eliah Riggs and Senator Bright. It is now altered by a mansard roof and victorian detail.

## 31st STREET
### (Formerly Congress Street)

1226—Small two story and dormered attic dwelling of brick and frame construction.

1644—TUDOR PLACE. 1802-1816. (See detailed account, page 88).

## POTOMAC STREET

1217, 1219, 1220, 1221, 1222, 1223, 1225—Simple brick two story dwellings. ca. 1820.

## 33rd STREET
### (Formerly Market Street)

1430—THE YELLOW HOUSE.
According to legend some part of this two story and attic structure, which is most apparently of early Nineteenth Century construction, was built on "Knaves Disappointment" before 1733 when it was willed to John Gordon. With a small garden to the left the door opens into a stair hall with two generous rooms to the right. To the rear, rooms extend on different levels. Several doors are of early type; flat on one side and full paneled on the other.

1501—A two story and dormer house. ca. 1810. Much altered in restoration.

1511-1513-1515-1517—Four small brick houses of two stories and dormered attic. Built ca. 1820. Restored.

1516—Same type as the above. Interesting ornate door. ca. 1820. Restored.

1520—A small two story brick house.

1524—THE YELLOW TAVERN. ca. 1795.
Also known as "The White House" this small house built of Flemish bond with white trim has a fine doorway probably taken from another dwelling and added later.

1540—A tiny two story brick house. ca. 1810.

1562-1564—Two small brick houses of two stories with attic dormers. Probably built about 1810.

1616-1620—Small brick houses somewhat altered in restoration.

## 34th STREET
### (Formerly Frederick Street)

1310—Small brick house, probably ca. 1820, considerably enlarged when restored.

1314—Small frame house, probably ca. 1820.
Southwest corner of O Street. Originally a fine square house built about 1800—now a store, it is enlarged and regrettably altered.

1406—A handsome brick house built before 1820 of ell shape, somewhat altered in restoration.

1411—A two story dwelling with dormered attic. It is enlarged and restored with a lovely walled garden. ca. 1810.

3410—VOLTA PLACE.
Slave quarters converted into two tiny frame cottages.

## 35th STREET
### (Formerly Fayette Street)

1307—A simple two story dwelling.

1404—A three story and attic house, ca. 1800.   Recently restored.

The Church—Convent of the Visitation, ca. 1800.


## RESERVOIR ROAD
### (Formerly Seventh Street)

3330—A simple two story frame house with dentiled cornice.   Built ca. 1800, and now much enlarged.

\*     \*     \*     \*     \*

# BIBLIOGRAPHY
### (Selected from over 500 References)

Adams, James Thurlow, The Epic of America.

Bayard, Margaret, A Winter in Washington, or Memoirs of the Seymour Family, published in 1824.

Brown, Glenn, Papers on the Improvement of Washington City.

Bryan, W. B., A History of the National Capital—Library of the National Archives F 194, B9 VI.

Century Magazine, April 1897, pp. 803-920.   Article entitled "Old Georgetown—A Social Panorama."

Clark, Allen C., Life and Letters of Dolly Madison.

Columbia Historical Society Records, V18, pp. 70-92:
    1—Old Homes on Georgetown Heights by William A. Gordon.
    2—Mackall Square.
    3—Doctor and Mrs. William Thornton by Allen C. Clark, p. 144.

Columbia Historical Society Records, V33-34, pp. 133-162.

Columbia Historical Society Records, V8, p. 195.   An Article on the Question of imported bricks, by George Alfred Townsend.

Cunningham, Younger & Smith, Georgian Architecture in the District of Columbia.

Ecker, Grace Dunlop, A Portrait of Old Georgetown.

Evans, Henry R., Old Georgetown on the Potomac.

Frary, I. T., They Built the Capitol.
    Lib. Cong. NA 4411. F7.   (A valuable chronology of Events through the building of the Capitol, beginning with the earliest plans.)

Great Georgian Houses of America, Vols. I and II.

Jackson, Richard P., The Chronicles of Georgetown, D.C., from 1751 to 1878.

Kimball, Fiske, Regional Types in Early American Architecture.

Leech, Margaret, Reveille in Washington.

Morris, Gouverneur, Diary.

National Geographic Magazine, April 1937.   Article by Dr. W. A. R. Goodwin, Rector of Bruton Parish.   "The Restoration of Colonial Williamsburg" (Problems and solutions parallel to those in other Tidewater restorations.)

Smith, Wilmer J., Measured Drawings of Georgian Architecture in the District of Columbia.

## BIBLIOGRAPHY (*Continued*)

Taggart, Hugh Thomas, Old Georgetown.

The Restoration of Colonial Williamsburg in Virginia.

Tolbert, Alice Coyle, Doorways and Dormers of Old Georgetown.
  Lib. Cong. F202 Gs T67.  (Guide book, with interesting map locating old houses.)

U. S. Catholic Historical Society, George-Town-on-the-Potowmack, 1931.  Historical records and studies.  V20, pp. 158-165.

Washington, D. C., A Guide to the National Capital (WPA American Guide Series.)

Washington, George, Diary.

Washington, George, Letters.

Waterman, Thomas Tileston, English Antecedents of Virginia Architecture.
  Lib. Cong. NA 730, V8 W3 Pamphlet Form.

Waterman, Thomas Tileston, Domestic Architecture of Tidewater Virginia.
  Lib. Cong. NA 7235 V5 W3 fol. Descriptions of houses.

Wilsbach, Paul, Tidewater Maryland.